GREAT BRITISH HOUSES

THE ANGLOPHILE'S GUIDEBOOK TO BRITAIN'S STATELY HOMES

Other Books by Anglotopia

101 Budget Britain Travel Tips
101 London Travel Tips
101 UK Culture Tips
Anglotopia's Guide to British Slang
Londontopia's Guide to Cockney Slang
Great Britons: Top 50 Greatest Brits
Great Events in British History
Great British Houses

Other Books by Jonathan Thomas

Adventures in Anglotopia
Anglophile Vignettes
Visions of Anglotopia
End to End: Britain From Land's End to John O'Groats

GREAT BRITISH HOUSES

THE ANGLOPHILE'S GUIDEBOOK TO BRITAIN'S STATELY HOMES

By
Anglotopia

Copyright © 2024 by Anglotopia LLC
Cover Design by Anglotopia LLC
Cover Copyright © 2024 Anglotopia LLC

Anglotopia LLC supports the right to free expression and the value of copyright. The purpose of copyright is to encourage writers and artists to produce the creative works that enrich our culture.

The scanning, uploading, and distribution of this book without permission is a theft of the author's intellectual property. If you would like permission to use material from the book (other than for review purposes), please contact info@anglotopia.net. Thank you for your support of the author's rights.

Anglotopia Press - An Imprint of Anglotopia LLC
www.anglotopia.press

Printed in the United States of America

1st US Edition: April 1st, 2023

Published by Anglotopia Press, an imprint of Anglotopia LLC.
The Anglotopia Press Name and Logo is a trademark of Anglotopia LLC.

Print Book interior design by Jonathan Thomas, all fonts used with license.

All location photographs © Jonathan Thomas
All other photos and art used in this book are in the public domain in the USA or in the Creative Commons.

Print ISBN: 978-1-955273-34-3

TABLE OF CONTENTS

Introduction..1
Goodwood House..15
Wollaton Hall...21
Abbotsford..27
Basildon Park..33
Burghley House...39
Anglesey Abbey..45
Kimbolton Castle...51
Wilton House..57
The Wardour Castle..63
Kedleston Hall..71
Forde Abbey...77
The Greenway Estate...83
Sudeley Castle..89
Dunham Massey...95
Polesden Lacey..101
Luton Hoo..107
Petworth House...113
Calke Abbey...119
Warwick Castle..125
Cliveden House..131
Bolsover Castle..137
Holkham Hall...143
Audley End..149
Beaulieu Palace House...155
Chequers...161
Brympton D'Evercy..167
Balmoral Castle..173
Bletchley Park..179
Waddesdon Manor..185
Leeds Castle..191

Chartwell..197
Osborne House..203
Hever Castle...209
Lyme Park..215
Woburn Abbey...221
Longleat...227
Dyrham Park..233
Stourhead...239
Highclere Castle...247
Castle Howard...253
Hardwick Hall..259
Blenheim Palace...265
Chatsworth..271
Wokefield Park...279
Alnwick Castle..283
Kingston Lacy..289
Knole House..295
Berkeley Castle..301
Wentworth Woodhouse...307
St Michael's Mount..313

INTRODUCTION

It's weird how you remember things and the assumptions you make about yourself. When I began brainstorming the introduction to this book, I thought that stately homes had played a big role in all my travels to England. It turns out that despite the oversized presence these great homes have in our public and private imaginations, I had not actually visited a proper stately home until my eighth trip to Britain. My first stately home was Blenheim Palace (though a day earlier, we visited Kelmscott, which is not a stately home, but a large house nonetheless). I could have sworn I'd visited a great house earlier than that!

Thanks to TV and movies, many of us associate the 'Great Country Houses' with England, and it helps us build our conception of all things English. Not only with great architecture but also with culture and history. An English Country House at the height of the British aristocracy was a microcosm of English life, much like a Royal Navy ship was a microcosm of England on the high seas. All human drama would take place in these houses, and there are thousands upon thousands of stories from the people who have worked, lived, and died in them.

So, of course, it's fertile ground for movies and TV shows.

The rise of Anglotopia in 2007 coincided with the rise of Downton Abbey soon after as the most popular period drama on the planet. We all became entranced by the trials and tribulations of the Crawley family, who inhabited a classic-sounding English house in Yorkshire called Downton Abbey. Highclere Castle, on the Hampshire/Berkshire Border, where the show was filmed, instantly became the most recognizable grand English house on the planet.

As Anglotopia developed, it made sense for us to commission a series of articles on Britain's great houses. Slowly, over a few years, we published fifty articles, each on what we considered the greatest and most important houses in Britain. When we started, fifty seemed like a lofty number, and we'd never reach it. By the time we got to the end of the first fifty, we realized the series could go on indefinitely! There are so many houses we haven't covered yet. However, the core of these fifty houses has remained on the website for almost a decade. Last year, in late 2023, we set about updating them and compiling them into this special little book.

So, before we dive into the fifty chapters of this book, I thought it would be fun to talk about four stately homes in England that have a special place in my heart.

First Stately Home - Blenheim Palace

My first stately home was Blenheim Palace, located in lovely, green Oxfordshire. While there are many excellent reasons to visit this magnificent example of Baroque architecture, my primary reason was simply that Sir Winston Churchill was born there, and I wanted to make a pilgrimage to where he was born (and subsequently, where he was buried nearby in Bladon).

Churchill's birth in this special place was not a coincidence. His father, Randolph Churchill, was the second son of the Duke of Marlborough, and Randolph and his young American wife Jennie, were frequent visitors. His birth there set a certain standard in his life and helped create his own conception of himself and his grand role in British history. It was the source of his family's history, its status in modern Britain, and his own sense of self. Blenheim Palace was England to Churchill. So, it made sense that he returned to it all throughout his life, and important milestones took place there (such as proposing to Clementine in the gardens).

The Churchill family's history with Blenheim, of course, goes back much, much further. Blenheim Palace was built for John Churchill, the first Duke of Marlborough, as a gift from Queen Anne and a thank-you for his victory over the French in the Battle of Blenheim in 1704. The palace was designed by Sir John Vanbrugh and Nicholas Hawksmoor, and it took 17 years to complete. It was intended to be a symbol of British power and prestige, and it remains one of England's most impressive stately homes to this day. It's the only non-royal, non-ecclesiastical Palace in Britain.

We visited in 2012 during a trip we took to Britain as a young family for the Queen's Diamond Jubilee. Visit Oxfordshire invited us to visit the Oxfordshire Cotswolds, and I knew immediately that I wanted to visit Blenheim Palace, so they were kind enough to arrange it. So, on a sunny June day, my wife and I visited with our six-month-old son in a stroller (I do not recommend doing this, you're better off using a baby wrap or other carrier).

Walking through the house and seeing the room where Churchill was born was a moving experience. I imagined young Churchill running around the hallways playing solider. In a glass case at the entrance are his toy soldiers. The house is a monument to the 1st Churchill, John Churchill, but now it's also become a monument to this second, possibly more famous Churchill, who saved Britain in another foreign war. There's now an ongoing special exhibition dedicated to Winston; the house uses the connection of its most famous son in all its marketing and advertising. Churchill Society conferences have been held there.

On a future trip, my second to visit Blenheim, I took a private tour of the Duke's apartments and got a behind-the-scenes look at life in the great house. It was fascinating to see how the place still functions as a playground for the rich and famous, much as it always has. Despite still being a private home, the house is now owned by a trust, so it must be opened to the public. But it's such a massive house that large parts of it can still be walled off from the visiting hordes. On that same visit, I attended a Battle Proms concert that was set up on the lawn in front of the house. The estate is a center of cultural life in Oxfordshire, and it's not uncommon for locals to visit several times a year (and you can usually get a yearly visiting pass for the price of one ticket).

My most recent visit to Blenehim was in 2022 when I visited for the first time since the pandemic. I was staying in Oxford for a summer course, so I decided to take the bus up on one of my free afternoons. The bus literally dropped me off at the gate, and I walked the almost one-mile-long driveway to the entrance. I toured the great staterooms once again and visited Churchill's birth room, where there was a special exhibition of his paintings, some rarely seen. I'll always take an opportunity to see his paintings as he was actually a very talented painter (you can't really say the same for other world leaders who've taken up the brush to imitate him).

After walking through the house and looking at the even newer exhibition dedicated to Churchill (with lovely artifacts on display), I walked the gardens and grounds around the house. It was a sunny, glorious July day, and that added to its splendor. I imagined Chruchill running around these gardens as a child and playing hide and seek with his cousins or his nanny. Or I imagined him much older, gingerly walking through the grounds with the love of his life. Then, inevitably, thoughts turn to how he must have felt walking through these grounds during Britain's darkest times (if he had even had the time to do so). There are historical rumors that Hitler ordered Oxford protected from bombing by the Luftwaffe because he wanted to make it the capital of a conquered Britain. It's not clear if that is completely true, but it's believable enough. If it were true, then Blenheim Palace, the birthplace of their sworn enemy, would have made an interesting trophy.

But that didn't happen. All because of the man who was born in those walls. The man who led Britain to victory with his visionary leadership and his inspiring words. It made perfect sense that he wished to be buried there at the source of his British greatness rather than at his beloved Chartwell. I will visit again and again.

Stourhead - My Local Stately Home

Longtime readers of Anglotopia will know that I have a special connection to Shaftesbury, a small town in Northern Dorset (that's practically almost in Wiltshire), because of a poster I once had hanging on my wall. It's the one place in England that I have visited the most over the years. If I were to retire to an English cottage one day, it would be to one in this special place. There are several grand houses and castles in the vicinity of Shaftesbury, but the most important one internationally, and my favorite by far, is Stourhead.

We first visited on that same Diamond Jubilee trip, and I immediately regretted not visiting sooner on our previous visits to Shaftsbury; it was just down the road! Stourhead is most well known for its gardens. You will recognize the gardens if you're a fan of British period films because they have been in several films, most notably the 2005 version of Pride and Prejudice (the rain scene is at the Temple of Apollo in the gardens where Darcy and Elizabeth argue). The gardens are truly splendid. We go more into this in the chapter on the place, but they are an 'English Arcadia' - the perfect ideal English landscape, and people come from all over the world to look at them.

For many, the house is a bit of an afterthought. Many might not even realize there is a house there because it is set back from the gardens, and you can't really see the house when you're walking around the carefully planned landscape. It's not even open all the time, so often the gardens are open, but the house is closed. But I love the house, and it's one of my favorites. It's not a massive place like Blenheim Palace; it's more modest, but you can still call it a grand house. Built in the Palladian style by the wealthy Bankes family (a banking family, and when it was built, considered 'new' money), the house is a statement of Georgian wealth and power (the house was burned in the early 1900s but rebuilt almost exactly as it was).

All of my visits to this special place have blended together over the years. I've lost count of how many times I've been there, how many times I've walked through the house and the gardens. How many times have I had tea in the cafe or browsed the gift shop?

It is the one National Trust property in Britain that I have been to the most and will return to time and time again.

My favorite visit, though, was back when Anglotopia used to publish a magazine, and we were invited to take a behind-the-scenes tour of Stourhead House. We arrived before the place had even opened and got the distinct pleasure of knocking on the front door as if we were visiting someone there. The great wooden door opened, and we were greeted by a curation specialist at the house. She proceeded to take us on the most personal, memorable tour of a stately home you could ever ask for. Not only did they guide us through all the staterooms, but we got to go upstairs and visit the parts of the house that the public doesn't normally get to see. I'll never forget passing through the attic rooms filled with furniture and artifacts, ghostly covered in sheets, awaiting their day to go on display. The best part was going into the crypt of the house and exploring the basement. We even got to see the wine cellar, which had spoiled wine from centuries ago untouched in place.

Stourhead is a special place in Anglotopia's heart, and I'll always be sure to stop by when I'm in the neighborhood. In fact, when I returned to Britain in 2022 after a four-year absence, it was one of the first places I visited after arriving in Shaftesbury.

Calke Abbey - My Favorite Stately Home

Despite visiting there so often, Stourhead is not my favorite stately home in England. No, my favorite is a place I've only been to once.

No place with an entry in the official National Trust guidebook is truly a secret, but when you arrive at Calke Abbey in Derbyshire, you very much feel like you're passing into another realm and into the pages of a legend. This treasure of Britain's national heritage is kept in a state of 'arrested decay' as it was when it was given to the Trust in the 1980s. What resulted was a time capsule of 20th-century aristocratic decline and a truly special place, a secret place, that we can all experience.

Arrival at Calke Abbey is down a long driveway, several miles in length. Past the gates to the estate, deep in the English countryside,

you're given a CD by the security guard at the entrance (this was in 2016; I'm not sure if they still do this). This CD tells you a story – it frames the secret place, and it's perfectly timed to the drive along the single-lane track leading to the house. Only you have no idea the house is actually there. Amongst fallen trees and endless rolling green hills, it's difficult to tell if there is a house here at all. And you begin to wonder if the National Trust is pulling your leg.

Eventually, you come around a bend, and there it is, sitting in the landscape, a silent sentry to history. Calke Abbey stands on the site of a 12th-century Augustinian priory and is a typical English Neoclassical state home built in the 1700s by the eccentric Harpur-Crewe family. Despite the word Abbey in its name, it was never an ecclesiastical building. It sits perfectly in the landscape, and for hundreds of years, the reclusive Harpur-Crewe family kept this view entirely to themselves, keeping the estate cut off from the world.

In their isolation, they filled the house with... well, the detritus that a family builds up for hundreds of years when it lives in the same building.

This house is 100 Years of Solitude by Gabriel Garcia-Marquez in actual reality. Every room is packed to the gills with stuff. Most of it left as it was when the National Trust took over the house in the 1980s. The family came to the end of the line in the 1980s, their isolation no longer tenable in a house that was crumbling around them. In lieu of crippling death duties, they gave the house to the National Trust.

Normally, when this happens, an army would descend upon the place and restore the house to its former glory, the way it was meant to be experienced in its golden age. The National Trust decided to do it differently with Calke Abbey, and they left it as they found it. It is in a state of permanent 'arrested decay' (though fear not, they still clean and preserve everything regularly). Walking through the house is to walk through a 300-year-old time capsule of English aristocracy. Rooms are filled with random things, wallpaper peeling off the walls, and paint chips on the ground.

The whole place has the most wonderful smell, a combination of dust, leather, and stale air. The clock has been stopped; the time machine has reached its destination. And now, this is a place that we

can enjoy, a sad, crumbling place that's a symbol of the decline of the British aristocracy in the 20th century. A sign in the café states that Calke Abbey is a 'secret place, where time stands still.' And it does. This is, by far, my favorite National Trust house.

Visit as soon as you can.

Stumbling Upon Darlington Hall

Have you ever been to a place that you've never been to before, but it looks very familiar to you - almost like you HAD been there before? A place that had become a part of you through a favorite book or film? And not realize what that place was until you were standing in front of it?

The Cotswolds in England are known for their picturesque countryside and quaint villages, but nestled amongst it all is a hidden gem: Dyrham Park. This stately home is a marvel of Baroque architecture, sitting comfortably in its landscape and showing its age with elegance. The honey-colored stone glows in the sunlight, and a stream runs fast alongside the driveway, creating a soothing atmosphere.

One winter day, my family and I stumbled upon Dyrham Park while searching for something to do. We were on the edge of the Cotswolds, and the National Trust app told us there was a stately home nearby. It was a stroke of luck that we found Dyrham Park, as we had no idea what to expect. As we walked down the drive towards the house, I had a feeling of familiarity. Had I seen this house before?

And then it clicked with me. This was the house from the film "The Remains of the Day," one of my all-time favorite British films. I was standing in front of Darlington Hall without realizing it. The sunny weather had perhaps led to my memory confusion, or maybe I never really gave much thought to Darlington Hall being a real place. But the house was there, and it was stunning.

The Remains of the Day is my favorite British film and one of my favorite books as well. I watch it several times a year. Its elegiac story about a butler in a great stately home in its final declining days is timeless and endlessly fascinating. It was quite something to be standing in front of it. When I picked the place to visit in the app, I didn't realize I was going to Darlington Hall! I do love a bit of travel serendipity.

We were the only visitors that day, and it felt like we were trespassing on someone's private home. The house was closed due to the terrible storms that had hit Britain that winter, but we decided to have a wander around anyway as the grounds were open. Some of grounds were flooded, and the drains were overflowing, but the beauty of the place shone through. The view of the sublime green rolling hills beyond the house was breathtaking, even in the winter.

Dyrham Park may be showing its age, but it's well taken care of by the National Trust. The stonework has borne the weathering of time, and it looks like it has always been there. It was the epitome of an English stately home, not too grand, but perfectly at home in its surroundings. As we left, I half expected the butler, Mr. Stephens, to walk out of the front door and enquire as to why we were trespassing on Lord Darlington's property.

Dyrham Park is a hidden treasure in the Cotswolds, and I feel lucky to have stumbled upon it. It's a place of history and beauty, and I can't wait to visit again one day (in fact, I've been there since, and it was just as lovely the second time!). Now, I think it's time to rewatch The Remains of the Day this weekend!

GOODWOOD HOUSE
The Home of the Festival of Speed

Key Facts

- Goodwood Country House is located in West Sussex, England.
- The house was originally built in the year 1600 as a hunting lodge.
- Goodwood House was dramatically extended in 1800 by James Wyatt.
- Today, Goodwood House is owned by the Dukes of Richmond and Gordon
- Now home to the iconic Festival of Speed

Goodwood House is primarily a 19th-century regency-style palace that has gone through a series of major remodels and extensions since the year 1600. With an art collection that has its origins in the Royal House of Stuart and famously unusual and decadent interiors, Goodwood House is nevertheless a modern English country house complete with a golf course, cricket ground, and annual festival of speed.

The Jacobean Earl of Northumberland built the first Goodwood House in the year 1600. A fairly unremarkable Jacobean gentleman's house, it was acquired by Charles Lennox, the 1st Duke of Richmond, natural son of King Charles II, and his French mistress Louise de Keroualle in 1697.

This original 'old house,' as it is now known, was extended and improved throughout the 18th century. In 1730, the main hall was redesigned by architect Roger Morris, known for his work on the Chichester Assembly Rooms, and between 1747 and 1750, the house was given a Palladian-style south wing by architect Matthew Brettingham, known for his work on Holkham Hall. In the early 19th century, a complementary north wing was added by architects James Wyatt and John Nash, who also added Regency State Apartments and towers to the south wing.

Goodwood House is now a villa-style regency palace built over two floors with picturesque domed towers and an exterior of grey stone and flint. The addition of these two wings and other major extensions carried out by Wyatt and Nash during the years 1800-1806 created Goodwood House's unique shape that resembles three sides of an octagon. The additional wing and ranges ordered by the 3rd Duke of Richmond were needed, in part, to house his extensive picture collection, most of which was salvaged from a fire at the family's London Home Richmond House in 1791.

Goodwood Country Estate reaches across almost 12,000 acres of beautiful Sussex Downs, and over the years, the various Dukes of Richmond in charge of the estate have modified and added to the gardens and estate. Cork oak trees and cedars of Lebanon planted by the 2nd Duke in 1740 still survive in areas around the house. The 3rd Duke added a thousand more trees to the gardens at Goodwood, a tennis court, and a walled garden before embarking on his most magnificent addition of a glamorous classical stable block designed by Sir William Chambers and, later, dog kennels designed by James Wyatt.

The rear entrance to Goodwood House takes the visitor through the Long Hall of the old Jacobean House, where Lion and Lioness by Stubbs and two of Canaletto's Thames landscapes, all formerly housed at Richmond House, hang. At the same time, the ambassador for France, the 3rd Duke of Richmond, acquired a set of magnificent Gobelin tapestries and had a room behind the hall built especially to house them. The Tapestry Room has been the setting of more Royal Privy Council meetings than any other private house.

Moving into the Wyatt wings, the music room features a fireplace by William Kent, also taken from Richmond House. The

English artist George Stubbs stayed at Goodwood for nine months in 1759 and painted prolifically during his stay. The fruits of his labor can be seen in the many hunting scenes on the walls of the front hall of Goodwood House.

The most famous room at Goodwood is undoubtedly its curious and extraordinary Egyptian Dining Room. In the late 18th century, Napoleon's Nile campaign led to an influx of Egyptian antiquaries and collectibles in Great Britain. Designed in 1802 by Wyatt, the Egyptian Dining Room is flamboyantly furnished, with statues, friezes, paintings, and even the fireplace, invoking ancient Egypt and the era of Cleopatra.

This room, amongst others, fell into decline and was drastically altered during the Victorian years, but the current owners, the Earl and Countess of March and Kinrara, completed a careful restoration of Goodwood's interiors, taking the home back to its original Regency appearance. One of the most spectacular examples of the Regency style is the Yellow Drawing Room, which features bright yellow silk drapes and royal portraits by the likes of Romney, Ramsay, and Mengs.

Horse Racing has been taking place at Goodwood for over two centuries. Goodwood Racecourse was established in 1802 and currently hosts the annual Glorious Goodwood meeting. Almost one hundred years after the racecourse was completed, a golf course designed by James Braid was commissioned and built on the grounds of Goodwood. Chichester/Goodwood Airport was built in the estate during World War II, and the internationally recognized Goodwood Motor Circuit was founded by the 9th Duke of Richmond in 1948. Goodwood House, Its grounds, and Motor Circuit have hosted the annual Goodwood Festival of Speed since 1993.

What Makes Goodwood Famous?

Goodwood House is a historic English country house given a modern-day twist. Home to an annual 'Festival of Speed' and complete with a racecourse, golf course, cricket ground, and grandstand, Goodwood House is where the upper classes come to play. An unusual house in design, Goodwood dates back to the year 1600 and has been the seat of the Duke of Richmond since 1697. With a family art collection that has its origins in the Royal House of Stuart and that infamous Egyptian Dining Room, Goodwood House is a fascinating historic building.

Goodwood House on Film and TV

Goodwood Racecourse and wider estate have featured in the following films and TV shows.

- The Man from U.N.C.L.E. (2015) Film
- Twice Around the Clock (2014) Documentary
- And When Did You Last See Your Father? (2007) Documentary
- Sports in Merrie, England (1913) Documentary
- Race for the Goodwood Cup (1908) Documentary
- Glorious Goodwood (1906) Documentary
- King Edward at Goodwood (1906) Documentary

Further Research

- James Peill (2013) The English Country House
- Jeremy Musson (2011) English Country House Interiors
- Rosemary Baird (2007) Goodwood: Art, Architecture, Sport and Family

Visiting Goodwood House

From 16th March to 13th October, Goodwood House is open to the public on most Sundays and Mondays. From the 4th to the 28th of August, the house is open five days a week, from Sunday to Thursday. Admission charges are £9.50 for adults, £4 for young people, and children under 12 go free.

Getting there by Train: There is a regular service from London Victoria to Chichester (1 hour, 40 minutes), plus the coastal service from Brighton and Portsmouth. Buses or taxis are available at Chichester Station.

Getting there by Road: Follow the A3 (Junction 10 on the M25) south towards Guildford. About 3 miles past Guildford, at the Milford turning, take the A283 to Petworth, then the A285 to Chichester for about 6 miles. Just beyond Upwaltham, turn right at the brown Goodwood sign. At the next Junction, turn left, following the brown sign to the hotel. The hotel entrance is a further 2 miles along on the right.

For more information, see the website www.goodwood.co.uk

WOLLATON HALL
A Home Fit for Batman

Key Facts about the House

- Wollaton Hall is located in Wollaton Park, Nottingham, England.
- Completed in 1588, Wollaton Hall was designed by architect Robert Smythson and built for Sir Francis Willoughby.
- Wollaton Hall opened to the public in 1926 and is home to Nottingham's Natural History Museum.

At the time Wollaton Hall was built, it was an architectural sensation. A decadent Elizabethan palace that showed stark Tudor England how to embrace the excesses of the Renaissance, Wollaton boasts the most dramatic facade of any English house built in the 16th century. Owned by the Willoughby family for 345 years, Wollaton Hall is now a Natural History Museum and is known for featuring in the Batman film The Dark Knight Rises as the exterior of Wayne Manor.

Wollaton Hall was built between 1580 and 1588, and the plans for the design were drawn up by architect Robert Smythson, who was heavily influenced by Dutch and German architecture. Smythson's floor plan for Wollaton is said to be inspired by da Majano's Villa Poggio Reale near Naples and de Lyra's reconstruction of Solomon's Temple in Jerusalem. Smythson's creation was a monster of parterres and terraces, an experimental palace that set the bar for the Baroque designs that were to follow almost a century later.

The man of the house, Sir Francis Willoughby, made his fortune in Nottinghamshire Coal. Legend has it that Willoughby was an eccentric man, an exacting and temperamental tycoon who had a habit of paying his workers in carts of the black stuff. It took eight years to build Wollaton Hall, which is situated at the top of a small hill that overlooks Willoughby's modest ancestral home. The material of choice for Wollaton was Ancaster stone from Lincolnshire, and it is thought that the master masons who worked on the building were brought over from Italy.

The central hall at Wollaton is cavernous and features a painted ceiling and wall by Antonio Verrio or possibly his assistant, Laguerre. Four towers guard each corner of the hall that rises to a glass-sided gallery where Nottinghamshire's oldest pipe organ can be found. The organ is thought to have been made at the end of the 17th century by builder Gerard Smith. The belvedere that rises above the medieval, yet flamboyant, hall offers views across Wollaton's five hundred acres of gardens and parkland to the city beyond.

A fire at Wollaton in the early 17th century caused extensive damage to Smythson's interiors. Under Lord Middleton, Wyatville was employed in 1801 to remodel Wollaton's interiors in his Windsor Castle style, a task he undertook intermittently for the next thirty years. Wyatville's central hall survives, featuring a classical stone screen and fake hammer-beam roof. Only one other room has been restored to the glory of the Wyatville design, and that's the Regency Dining Room, where visitors can enjoy a video of a former Wollaton housekeeper.

Other restored rooms include the kitchens, which have been fitted as a working Tudor kitchen using an inventory that dates to 1601, and the Regency Salon, which is presented as it would have looked in 1862 when Lady Jane Middleton was still in residence. From the date it was completed in 1588 until the year 1811, Wollaton Hall passed down through generations of the Willoughby Family. By 1881, the current owner of Wollaton Hall, Digby Willoughby, 9th Baron Middleton, decided that the growing city of Nottingham had expanded too close to his property. Seeking a more countryside location, Baron Middleton moved out and let the house to tenants.

Following a period of vacancy, Wollaton Hall was sold to Nottingham Council in 1924 and opened to the public in 1926. The council transformed Wollaton Hall into a Natural History Museum, housing some three-quarters of a million specimens related to zoology, botany, and geology. The house is segmented into six main exhibition areas: the National Connections Gallery, Bird Gallery, Insect Gallery, Mineral Gallery, Africa Gallery, and the Natural History Matters Gallery.

In 2007, Wollaton Hall reopened following a massive refurbishment, funded partly by the European Union Regional Development Fund and the Heritage Lottery Fund. As part of the renovation, the gardens and deer park were also landscaped and modified. Now, Wollaton Hall Park is regularly used for large outdoor events like festivals and concerts, and the exterior of the house has been used as a filming location for the Batman film The Dark Knight Rises.

What Makes Wollaton Hall Famous?

Wollaton Hall is famous for its flamboyant and imposing facade. An experimental and highly decorative Elizabethan mansion, Wollaton Hall was a sensation in its day. After spending nearly 350 years as the family home of the aristocratic Willoughby family, Wollaton Hall is now known for being Nottingham's Natural History Museum and features reconstructed historical rooms.

Wollaton Hall in TV and Film

- Heart of Chaos (2015)
- The Dark Knight Rises (2012)
- Crossroads (2001 TV series)
- Treasure Hunt (1982)

Further Research

- Sheila Strauss (1978) Short History of Wollaton and Wollaton Hall
- Robert Cullen and Pamela Marshall (1999) Wollaton Hall and the Willoughby Family
- Friedman (1988) House and Household in Elizabethan England: Wollaton Hall and the Willoughby Family

Visitor Information

Wollaton Hall and Natural History Museum is open to the public all year round. In high season, which runs from February to November, Wollaton Hall is open every day from 10 am until 5 pm. During low season, the hall and museum are open from Friday to Tuesday from 11 am until 4 pm. Entry is free, but there is a charge for tours.

Wollaton Hall is three miles west of Nottingham City Center. To travel to Wollaton Hall by train, go to Nottingham Central Train Station and take a local bus from the city center. If traveling by car from Nottingham City Center, follow the brown tourist signs from the A52 or A6514, or if arriving via the M1, take junction 25 and follow the signs.

ABBOTSFORD
The Ancestral Home of Sir Walter Scott

Key Facts about Abbotsford

- Abbotsford is located near Galashiels in the town of Melrose on the south bank of the River Tweed, Scotland.
- A category A listed building, Abbotsford belonged to Scottish novelist and poet Sir Walter Scott and was built in stages throughout the early 19th
- Abbotsford remained in the Scott family until 2004 and is now a popular historic country house and visitor attraction run by a charitable trust.

The ancestral home of Scotland's most famous literary son, Sir Walter Scott, Abbotsford is a popular tourist attraction in the Scottish borders. Abbotsford grew from humble beginnings into a grand, romantic mansion, an icon of 19th-century Scottish Baronial architecture. Once Sir Walter Scott's most cherished possession, his 'conundrum castle,' Abbotsford is now a museum and shrine to the great writer's life and work.

At first, Abbotsford was nothing more than a farmhouse and a modest estate of 100 acres known locally as Clarty Hole, a play on its official title of Cartleyhole. Sir Walter Scott purchased the scenic spot in 1811 to serve as his countryside home outside of Edinburgh. Initially, Scott built a small villa and named it Abbotsford after the abbots of Melrose Abbey, who used to cross the river Tweed via a nearby Ford. In his first few years at Abbotsford, Scott was preoccupied with acquiring more land and managed to increase his estate from 110 acres to 1400.

Soon, though, Scott's literary career and the fame and fortune that came with it gave him the funds to transform his humble farmhouse into a country mansion where he could live, work, and entertain in style. Scott never seemed to harbor dreams of building a grand mansion; rather, the Abbotsford we see today grew in gradual stages with the input of Scott's many friends, including some of Scotland's finest architects, craftsmen, and designers.

At first, Scott expanded his farmhouse with the help of architect William Atkinson and designer David Ramsay Hay, adding a study, a dining room, an armory, and a conservatory, with bedrooms and attic rooms on the floor above. Both architect and designer were to go on to do magnificent things as Atkinson was later responsible for the remodeling of Chequers and Ramsay Hay redecorated the Palace of Holyroodhouse for Queen Victoria.

This arrangement served the Scott family well for a few years, but by 1920, Scott was making more money than ever and began planning extensive building works with Atkinson. In 1822, the existing Abbotsford House was torn down to make way for the building of a new, large, rectangular house. Scott hired a local stonemason, Smiths of Darnick, to be the principal builder of the new Abbotsford and insisted that he integrated carved stones and wooden paneling from ruined abbeys and castles around Scotland to give it a strong link with the past. In the great entrance hall at Abbotsford, there is a stone fireplace carved by Smiths of Darnick and inspired by Scott's poem, The Lay of the Last Minstrel. The ceiling and walls in this room are dominated by suits of armor, carved oak paneling salvaged from Dunfermline Abbey, and the coats of arms and shields of Scott's ancestors.

Anyone familiar with Scott's work will be thrilled to take a look inside his study. The last room to be completed in Abbotsford, it is in this atmospheric, book-lined room that Scott penned his later novels including the nine-volume biography The Life of Napoleon Buonaparte. The drawing room at Abbotsford features beautiful Chinese hand-painted wallpaper, a gift from a relative of Scott's who worked for the East India Company, as well as the latest in domestic engineering; Abbotsford was one of the first homes in Scotland to be gas-lit and had air-bells fitted for summoning servants. Although a lover of technology, Scott was an antiquarian at heart and housed a large collection of arms, including his own military and sports weapons, in his purpose-built armory.

Scott's library at Abbotsford is one of Scotland's great treasures. Containing books and manuscripts that are completely unique, including several incunables (books written before 1,500) and almost 5,000 chapbooks, Abbotsford Library is the most impressive room in the house. The shelves at Abbotsford Library are a testament to the intellect and curiosity of the man who filled them, with sections devoted to history, geography, folklore, practical reference, and versions of Scott's own works in multiple languages.

Other rooms at Abbotsford that are open to visitors include the exhibition room, used as a breakfast parlor, the dining room in which Scott died following a series of strokes, and the unique religious corridor and Catholic chapel. Already a popular place of literary pilgrimage, just 20 years after Scott's death, Abbotsford was remodeled in the 1850s by Scott's granddaughter Charlotte. Charlotte married James Robert Hope, and the newlyweds created a dedicated tourist route through the most historic parts of the house in an attempt to separate their own private living space from Sir Walter Scott's many curious fans.

The last of the Scott clan to live in the house, Dame Jean Maxwell-Scott and her sister Patricia turned Abbotsford into one of Scotland's best tourist attractions during the years they looked after it and, on Dame Maxwell-Scott's death in 2004, passed it on to an independent charitable trust.

What Makes Abbotsford Famous?

Abbotsford House is one of the most famous houses in the world, particularly for lovers of literature. A monument to the life and work of the man who created it, the house at Abbotsford was the bricks-and-mortar love of Sir Walter Scott's life. Full of Scott's own antiquarian collections, Abbotsford is a museum, shrine, and iconic example of 19th-century Scottish Baronial style.

Abbotsford in TV and Film

- A History of Scotland (2008 TV series)
- Antiques Roadshow (1979 TV Series)
- Further Research
- Anonymous (2015) Abbotsford: Beautiful Britain Series
- Sheila Scott (2014) Abbotsford: building by numbers
- N. Wilson (2002) A Life of Walter Scott: The Laird of Abbotsford
- Mary Scott and William Gibb (1983) Abbotsford; the personal relics and antiquarian treasures of Sir Walter Scott

Visitor Information

Abbotsford's visitor center, restaurant, and estate paths are open to the public seven days a week, all year round. Abbotsford House and Gardens are also open all year round, but opening hours differ depending on the season. Entry fees apply, so visit the website for more information on opening times and prices: http://www.scottsabbotsford.com/visit/.

To get to Abbotsford from Edinburgh, take a bus to Carlisle via Galashiels. At Galashiels Bus Station, transfer to a local bus for Galafoot Bridge, 10 minutes walking distance via a public footpath to Abbotsford.

BASILDON PARK
A Georgian Masterpiece Saved from Wreck and Ruin

Key Facts about Basildon Park

- Basildon Park is located in Berkshire, England, between the villages of Upper Basildon and Lower Basildon.
- Designed by John Carr, Basildon Park was built between 1776 and 1783 for Sir Francis Syke.
- A Grade I listed building, Basildon passed into the ownership of the National Trust in 1978.

Used by the British army during both world wars, left derelict numerous times in history, and almost sold piece-by-piece to America, Basildon Park is a true survivor. Reborn in the 1950s, thanks to a loving and painstaking restoration by Lord and Lady Iliffe, Basildon Park is an authentic Georgian mansion that has managed, against all odds, to forge a place for itself in the 21st century.

Sir Francis Sykes was an ambitious man. Having made a vast fortune in India with the British East India Company, he returned to England determined to make his name in British politics. After buying two large estates and becoming a Member of Parliament, Sykes set his sights on the estate of Basildon and commissioned the building of a grand mansion designed by renowned architect John Carr of York.

In 1771, work on Basildon was due to begin, but Sykes's life took a dramatic turn for the worse, financially and politically, when

East India shares collapsed, and he was embroiled in a scandal over his work as a tax collector in Bengal. Work on Basildon did not begin until 1776 and, due to cash flow issues, lasted for the entirety of Sykes's life.

The architect in charge of the building of Basildon, John Carr of York, was heavily influenced by Palladian architecture. His layout of a central block flanked by pavilions and a long, three-storied west front is thought to have been based on drawings of Palladio's Villa Emo. At the time Basildon was being built, neoclassicism, typified by the work of Robert Adams, was rising in popularity, and Carr employed the austerity of this style in Basildon's east front.

Carr's interiors are a refined yet dramatic homage to Robert Adam, with whom he had previously worked on the interiors at Fairfax House. The hall, which remains to this day as Carr left it, features Etruscan ceiling panels and wall medallions with delicate plasterwork picked out in pastel shades. An entrance hall leads to a staircase that opens out into the Octagon Saloon with large Venetian windows that complement the vista of the park beyond. It is in the dining room that we can most clearly see Carr's admiration of Adams; a screen of columns dominates one end of the room, and the ceiling is decked out with a wheel of tendrils featuring the heads of Roman emperors.

On Sykes's death in 1804, Basildon passed into the hands of his son, who died within weeks and passed the house on to his son, five-year-old Sir Francis Sykes. As a child, the third Baronet was an acquaintance of the Prince Regent, a friendship that proved to be incredibly costly as, at the age of just 14, Sykes entertained the Prince at Basildon.

In 1834, Prime Minister Benjamin Disraeli was a houseguest at Basildon. The arrangement was a peculiar one as, at the time, Disraeli was in the throes of a romantic affair with Sykes's wife Henrietta, a relationship he even wrote a book about, *Henrietta Temple: a Love Affair*. During this period, Basildon was on the market but not yet attracting any serious buyers.

Finally, in 1838, Basildon was sold to MP James Morrison, an old-fashioned self-made man who began his career as an assistant in a London Haberdashery. The property was passed down to his daughter, who was unmarried, and in 1910, it was passed to her nephew, also named James Morrison. A World War One veteran who served with distinction, Morrison lived in Basildon until 1929, when he was forced to sell for financial reasons.

In the succeeding years, it seems no one really knew what to do with old Basildon. The 1st Lord Iliffe purchased the estate only to remove the doors and fireplaces and put it straight back on the market. Property developer George Ferdinando came next. His master plan was to sell Basildon to a wealthy American, have the whole building deconstructed, shipped to America, and re-built in a location of the new owner's choosing. Thankfully, this never happened, but the dining room fittings did make their way to the Waldorf-Astoria Hotel in New York to decorate their 'Basildon Room.'

During the Second World War, things only got worse for Basildon as the house was used as a soldier's billet and training ground and suffered a great deal of damage to its interiors and grounds, but salvation was just around the corner. In 1952, the 2nd Baron and Lady Iliffe purchased Basildon and set about a massive restoration that would take 25 years to complete. When Lady Iliffe arrived, army graffiti covered the walls, almost all of the windows were broken, the lead tiles had been stolen from the roof, and the whole property was in a sad state of disrepair.

Slowly and carefully, Lady Iliffe restored Basildon with salvaged 18th-century fixtures and fittings and purchased antique furniture and paintings to replace all that had been lost or destroyed, including a large collection of works by Batoni. In 1978, the Iliffe's passed Basildon into the hands of the National Trust and it has been enjoyed by visitors and used regularly as a historic filming location ever since.

What Makes Basildon Park Famous?

Basildon Park is famous for being one of the few houses of its kind to survive the impact of the 20th century on aristocratic life. A Georgian mansion that survived bankruptcy, two world wars, and the attentions of a wealthy American, Basildon Park was brought back from the dead as recently as the 1950s. Now a popular filming location and visitor attraction, Basildon Park is a truly great success story for English houses.

Basildon Park in TV and Film

- Downton Abbey (2013 TV series)
- The Royal Bodyguard (2011 TV series)
- Dorian Gray (2009)
- The Duchess (2008)
- Marie Antoinette (2006)
- Pride & Prejudice (2005)

Further Research

- National Trust (2002) Basildon Park.

Visitor Information

Basildon Park is maintained by the National Trust and is open to the public all year round. Visit the website for more information on opening times and entry fees. http://www.nationaltrust.org.uk/basildon-park

If visiting Basildon Park by train, the nearest train stations are Pangbourne train station and Goring train station. The park is around a 5-minute taxi ride from either of these stations. To get to Basildon Park by car, leave the M4 at exit 12 and follow signs for Beale Park and Pangbourne. There is parking available on site.

BURGHLEY HOUSE
An Elizabethan Marvel

Key Facts about Burghley House

- Burghley House is located near Stamford, Peterborough.
- Built between 1558 and 1587, Burghley was built for Sir William Cecil, Queen Elizabeth I's chief advisor and Lord High Treasurer.
- Burghley House has remained much as it was in Elizabethan times and is now owned by a preservation trust set up by descendants of Lord Burghley.

Burghley House is truly spectacular. An Elizabethan palace to which only actual royal residences can compare, Burghley House is the most magnificent house built during Queen Elizabeth's reign. Only the best for Queen Elizabeth's most faithful and long-serving advisor, Lord Burghley, who rose from the status of lawyer to become Queen Elizabeth I's chief advisor for most of her reign, Secretary of State, and Lord High Treasurer. Burghley House has been owned by the Cecil family since Elizabethan times.

Sir William Cecil began his career as a lawyer and, under the Protector Somerset, came to occupy one of the highest-ranking positions in Queen Elizabeth I's inner circle. Designed by Cecil himself, Burghley House came to symbolize all of the might and splendor of the Elizabethan court. Less a family home, more a small kingdom, Burghley was built to house the Cecil descendants, a powerful dynasty that has, since 1801, included the marquesses of Exeter.

Burghley's exteriors are a perfect example of sixteenth-century Elizabethan architecture, with its three facades reflecting the perfect symmetry of 16th-century design. The plan for Burghley began as an almost modest, by Elizabethan standards, medieval manor house with a courtyard following from a gatehouse and a porch giving access to the Great Hall. Soon, these plans were overwhelmed, and the floor plan of the house grew to create a letter E in honor of the Queen, while the main part of the house swelled to include 35 main rooms on the ground and first floors. There are also over 80 smaller rooms and scores of halls, bathrooms, and service areas in the rest of this sprawling palace, whose exterior is adorned with ostentatious porches and pennants and roof with a multitude of cupolas, pavilions, and chimneys.

Burghley was built gradually over the course of Lord Burghley's long career, and upon his death in 1598, most of the interiors were still undecorated and unfurnished. Most rooms remained bare until the house passed into the hands of the 5th Earl of Exeter and received its sensational makeover. The 5thEarl and his wife, Lady Anne Cavendish, were a well-traveled pair, and throughout the 1680s and 1690s, while Britain tried to remake itself following the Restoration, they indulged themselves in four Grand Tours of Europe. The seventeen rooms on the principal reception floor of Burghley are filled with the treasures amassed by the Earl and Lady Cavendish during this time. The rooms feature over 300 paintings, as well as tapestries, fine furniture, and sculptures. The overall effect of these lavish rooms is on par with one of Europe's finest museums or the state rooms of Windsor Castle itself.

In the rest of the house, the Grand tour collection continues with the chapel decorated with a work by Paolo Veronese, taken from a church on the Venice island of Murano. Similarly, the chapel's marble fireplace once adorned a church somewhere in Portugal. The state dining room marvels with an Anthony and Cleopatra wall mural by Laguerre, the brown drawing room features portraits by Gainsborough, and the black-and-yellow bedroom is home to exquisite carvings by Grinling Gibbons. For a look at the relationship that made all of this possible, wander to the Pagoda Room to see two paintings by Gheeraerts depicting Burghley and his Queen. Of course, Queen Elizabeth had her own bedroom in case she ever chose to come and stay, with the finest tapestries and bed hangings in the whole palace, but her only planned visit was prevented by an outbreak of smallpox in the area.

There wasn't much that could be done by subsequent generations to improve on what the 5th Earl did at Burghley, and little changed until the 9th Earl took control. By now, it was the mid-eighteenth century, and the 9th Earl of Exeter, Lord Burghley Brownlow Cecil, had furnished the official state rooms at Burghley House in honor of the first of the Hanoverians. Old Master paintings adorn the walls of what is often referred to as the George Rooms, which contains furniture by Boulle and a Piranesi fireplace. The two really unmissable rooms at Burghley House are, of course, Heaven and Hell. In one, a Roman temple shows us views of a beautiful sky, and in the other, the floor disappears into a dark staircase. The 9th Earl also enlisted Capability Brown, the leading landscape gardener of the day, to lay out the gardens at Burghley.

Today, Burghley House is run by a charitable trust headed by members of the Cecil family, but the Burghley title is currently held by the many-titled Michael Cecil, 8th Marquess of Exeter, 17th Earl of Exeter and 19th Baron Burghley.

What Makes Burghley House Famous?

There is nowhere quite like Burghley. The only great houses that can compare with Burghley's grandiose Elizabethan architecture and world-class grand tour collection are those that were built to house kings and queens. The treasures amassed by the 5th Earl of Exeter and Lady Cavendish during their multiple Grand Tours of Europe elevate Burghley from being just another fine country house to one of the most spectacular houses in England.

Burghley House in TV and Film

- Elizabeth: The Golden Age (2007)
- Da Vince Code (2006)
- Pride & Prejudice (2005)

- Bleak House (2005 mini-series)
- The Curious House Guest (2005 TV series)
- Middlemarch (1994 mini-series)

Further Research

- Lady Victoria Leatham (2000) Burghley House (Great Houses of Britain)
- R. Impey (1998) The Cecil Family Collects: Four Centuries of Decorative Arts from Burghley House
- Hugh Brigstoke (1995) Italian Paintings from Burghley House
- Lady Victoria Leatham (1999) Burghley: The Life of a Great House

Visitor Information

Burghley House is open to the public every day except Friday during the summer months. Admission charges as of 2015 are £13.50 for adults and £6.70 for children; for more details on opening hours and admission fees, see the website www.burghley.co.uk.

If visiting Burghley by train, the nearest train station is Stamford, a short taxi ride or a 30-minute walk to the entrance. Stamford station can easily be accessed from the London to Edinburgh mainline. If traveling by car, exit the A1 at Carpenters Lodge and follow the signs to Burghley House.

Image © By Stephen Turner

ANGLESEY ABBEY
A Stunning Country Home in Cambridgeshire

Key Facts about the House

- Anglesey Abbey is located in the village of Lode, a few miles from the city of Cambridge in England.
- A priory was built on the site of Anglesey Abbey between 1100 and 1135 and was converted into a country house around 1600.
- Anglesey Abbey now belongs to the National Trust and is open to the public.
- Notably, not on the Isle of Anglesey in Wales.

The origins of Anglesey Abbey date back to the 12th century, but Anglesey only became a house of real note in the 1920s when it was purchased by wealthy bachelor Huttleston Broughton. Broughton, later Lord Fairhaven, transformed this tired country house into a luxurious mansion in which to entertain the best of English society. Filling the mansion with his extensive art and antique collection, Fairhaven created a personal museum and gallery with landscaped gardens that are magnificent to behold.

The history of Anglesey Abbey is long and rather unremarkable. Originally built as a priory during Henry I's reign, Anglesey existed comfortably until the Dissolution of the Monasteries in 1535, at which time it was seized by the crown.

Anglesey Abbey first became a family home in 1600 when it was purchased by Thomas Hobson, who converted the abbey into a country house. A few structural features were saved from the original priory, including walls to the left and right of the main entrance, a few external arches, and the monk's parlor, which was converted into a dining room. In the late 18th century, Anglesey

Abbey passed into the hands of Sir George Downing, founder of Cambridge's Downing College. Downing carried out a series of improvements and alterations to Hobson's design, none of which remain today.

It wasn't until 1926, when Anglesey Abbey was purchased by Huttleston and Henry Broughton that the house and estate became a thing of real beauty. Huttleston Broughton's father, Urban Broughton, had gone to America as a young man on a mission to make a fortune, and in his marriage to a wealthy American heiress, he did just that. On Urban's death, Huttleston took on the barony intended for his father and became Lord Fairhaven.

Huttleston Broughton was educated at Harrow and Sandhurst and served as a lieutenant in the First World War. Following the war, Broughton is thought to have spent most of his time taking long yachting trips with his mother, shooting, and horse racing. At the age of thirty, the future Lord Fairhaven took on a dilapidated mansion amidst an uninspiring landscape and set about transforming it into the height of 1930s country house luxury.

Lord Fairhaven spent years transforming Anglesey Abbey, making improvements to the Elizabethan exterior, with its oriel windows and strong chimneys, and completely renewing its interiors. The only room to survive from Anglesey's days as an Augustine Abbey is a medieval vaulted crypt that became Lord Fairhaven's dining room. Using designer Sidney Parvin, other rooms in the house were medievalized, making copious use of tapestries and pictures evoking the Jacobean period. In keeping with Lord Fairhaven's intentions to use his home as a place to entertain shooting parties, the Victorian parlor at Anglesey was transformed into the Oak Room, a small drawing room with an elaborate plaster ceiling where guests could rest comfortably after a day spent racing or shooting.

Lord Fairhaven added both a library and an art gallery to Anglesey Abbey. The Library was completed in 1938 and contains his extensive collection of books as well as contemporary portraits of all the English monarchs. Gradually, the whole of Anglesey became a museum to Lord Fairfax's love of history and art. The walls of Anglesey are home to a Gainsborough seascape, a Constable, Claude Lorraine landscapes, and the Victorian nudes of William Etty.

As well as paintings, Lord Fairhaven collected tapestries from Bruges and Mortlake, Ming porcelain, silver, and an extensive collection of French and English clocks. A rolling ball clock by Wiliam Congrave and the 'Pagoda clock,' which is a working automaton, are just two treasures from this collection.

Lord Fairhaven also transformed the unpromising meadows around Anglesey, designing magnificent gardens with stately avenues and woodlands that stretch over 46 hectares. Classical statuary depicting scenes from mythology can be found all over the gardens, and the snowdrops that bloom here are said to be among the best in England.

Having spent much of the 20th century living the lifestyle of a wealthy 19th-century gentleman, Lord Fairhaven bequeathed Anglesey Abbey to the National Trust in 1966. Now, Anglesey Abbey House, Gardens, and the working watermill are popular visitor attractions.

What Makes Anglesey Abbey Famous?

Lord Fairhaven transformed Anglesey Abbey into a haven of 19th-century elegance, his own personal museum and art gallery with gardens that would rival those conceived by the famous Capability Brown. Here, Fairhaven hid away from the rapid change of 20th century England and continued to entertain his friends with shooting, horse racing, and parties, surrounded by fine works of art well into the swinging sixties. A time warp of a simpler time, carefully conserved by the National Trust and with some of the most beautiful winter gardens in England, Anglesey Abbey is a real English treasure.

Anglesey Abbey in TV and Film

- Treasure Hunt (1982 TV series)

Further Research

- National Trust (2002) Anglesey Abbey Guidebook
- National Trust (1997) Anglesey Abbey Gardens
- Mark Purcell and David Pearson (2013) Treasures from Lord Fairhaven's Library at Anglesey Abbey

Visitor Information

Anglesey Abbey is maintained by the National Trust and is open to the public. The gardens and restaurant at Anglesey are open year-round, but the opening times for the house differ depending on the season. Visit the website for more information on opening times and entry fees. http://www.nationaltrust.org.uk/anglesey-abbey/

If visiting Anglesey Abbey by train, the nearest station is Cambridge and Newmarket, 6 miles away. To get to Anglesey Abbey from Cambridge by car, use the B1102. Anglesey is signposted from the A14, Junction 35.

KIMBOLTON CASTLE
A Stunning Castle Turned Mansion in Cambridgeshire

Key Facts about Kimbolton Castle

- Kimbolton Castle is located in Kimbolton town in Huntingdonshire, Cambridgeshire.
- The first castle built on the site of Kimbolton Castle was erected around the year 1200 by Godfrey Fitzpiers, Earl of Essex
- Kimbolton Castle was converted into a stately palace in the 17th century and is now used as a public school.

A Norman castle, a Tudor manor house, a Georgian mansion, and finally, a public school. Kimbolton Castle has survived many centuries of change. The final resting place of Catherine of Aragon, Henry VIII's divorced and banished Spanish Queen, Kimbolton Castle, sits amidst wooded grounds close to the small town of Kimbolton. Kimbolton Castle is not generally open to the public, but it's worth visiting as part of a group tour for the lovingly restored and displayed historic interiors, Pellegrini murals, and dedicated heritage room.

The town of Kimbolton has had its own castle since Norman times. In the 11th century, a wooden motte and bailey were erected in Kimbolton, but all that remains of this castle is the mound of earth on which it stood. Soon after, around the year 1200, Lord of the Manor Geoffrey Fitzpiers built a fortified manor house on the site of the present Kimbolton Castle. This castle managed to survive the Middle Ages, with several owners and extensive building works, only to be demolished and rebuilt by the Wingfield family in the

1520s as a Tudor manor house.

Now Kimbolton Castle enters the history books. In April 1534, the Tudor manor house became the home of Queen Catharine of Aragon, earning itself a place in the fascinating saga of the reign of Henry VIII. Henry VIII's first wife was separated from her daughter Mary and sent to live at Kimbolton Castle as punishment for her refusal to recognize the King's denial of the validity of their marriage. Catherine would not recognize Henry's new wife, Anne Boleyn, as Queen of England and was held at Kimbolton from the time of her divorce until her untimely death.

The cause of Catherine of Aragon's death is unknown. Some have speculated that the fenland climate was enough to damage her already fragile health, while others have suggested that she succumbed to some form of cancer. Whatever the direct cause, Catherine of Aragon was a woman wronged, a political pawn separated from her daughter and rejected by her husband and king. Those wronged in life make vengeful ghosts, and Catherine of Aragon is said, to this day, to haunt the halls of Kimbolton Castle.

Catherine is not the only ghost said to haunt Kimbolton Castle. Around 1600, almost seventy years after Catherine's death, Sir John Popham, who became Lord Chief Justice and was famous for being the judge at the trial of Guy Fawkes, lived at Kimbolton Castle. Not only did Sir Popham die at Kimbolton, but he is said to have murdered his own baby daughter by throwing her from a window above the courtyard. Local legend claims Sir Popham's ghost stalks the grounds to protect his property from thieves. The Popham Gallery at Kimbolton Castle, located above the chapel, is named after this intriguing character.

Now, with a reputation as a haunted castle firmly established, Kimbolton was purchased by Henry Montagu, 1st Earl of Manchester, and remained in the Montagu family for the next 335 years. A large part of the castle collapsed in 1707, and Charles Edward Montagu, the 1st Duke of Manchester, carried out huge renovation works throughout the early 18th century. The Duke employed the services of architect Sir John Vanbrugh to transform the facades of the castle in a classical Baroque style, retaining the original castle battlements and Tudor and Stuart courtyard within. Remnants of the old Tudor castle can be seen all over what is now Kimbolton School. One side of the courtyard has Tudor brickwork featuring stone mullions, and in the basement, Tudor windows and Gothic windows can be seen, as well as the original chapel.

Vanbrugh's Baroque facade dominates Kimbolton, and evidence of his classical design can be seen all over the building's exterior. Drainpipes masked as palm trees, pilasters, and scrolls above windows and a magnificent doorway, similar to that at Hampton Court, adorn the exterior of the great hall. Vanbrugh's work on the saloon is among his most exquisite, with red walls, gilded pillars, and Louis XIV-inspired furnishing commissioned from French upholsterers. The state bedchamber and adjoining boudoir take up Catherine of Aragon's former rooms.

A portico was added to Kimbolton by Italian architect Alessandro Galilei, and celebrated Venetian artist Pellegrini painted murals on the chapel balcony and main staircase. The chapel is adorned with images of the saints, while the staircase features narrative scenes depicting the triumphs of Caesar and William III and musicians playing a fanfare from above. Robert Adam designed plans for additional buildings to adorn the gardens at Kimbolton, but only a gatehouse was ever constructed around the year 1764.

Like many of England's stately buildings, Kimbolton Castle was used during World War II and became a hospital for the Royal Army Medical Corps. In 1950, the 10th Duke of Manchester sold the castle, and it stands today as a public school, sometimes used for functions and as a television and film location.

What Makes Kimbolton Castle Famous?

A former medieval castle, rebuilt and renovated over the years to become an 18th-century manor house, Kimbolton Castle is one of many great houses of its kind that can be seen all over England. It could have been ordinary if it wasn't for one special guest, the work of Vanbrugh and Pellegrini, and a series of unhappy ghosts. Kimbolton Castle is now Kimbolton School, but it earned its place in history as the place where Catherine of Aragon died.

Kimbolton Castle in TV and Film

- Wolf Hall (2015)

Further Research

- John Michael Stratford (2002) From Churchyard to Castle: A History of Kimbolton School

Visitor Information

As Kimbolton Castle is still used as a school, it is not generally open to the public. However, requests for group tours can usually be accommodated during school holidays. The castle is open to the public one day per year. For dates and charges, please see the website, www.kimbolton.cambs.sch.uk

WILTON HOUSE
A Stunning Example of Palladian Architecture in Wiltshire

Key Facts about Wilton House

- Wilton House is located in Wilton, in the county of Wiltshire in England.
- There was a priory on the site of Wilton House from the year 871, but the present house was largely built around 1543 by William Herbert, 1stEarl of Pembroke.
- Wilton house is still in private ownership and is currently owned by the 18th Earl of Pembroke. It has been open to the public since 1951.

Wilton House is an impressive example of severe Palladian style and is home to Inigo Jones' famous Single and Double Cube Rooms, believed by some to be the finest 17th-century staterooms in England. Privately owned since King Henry VIII seized it from its resident nuns and handed it over to his brother-in-law, Wilton House contains a stunning collection of paintings and furniture and has been open to the public since 1951.

Truly one of the great houses of England, Wilton House began its life as a nunnery. The abbey at Wilton was built around 871 and founded by the first recognized Saxon sovereign of England, King Egbert. Under King Alfred, known later as Alfred the Great, who was known to be a devout Christian, the abbey grew until it became one of the most prosperous in England.

Of course, Wilton Abbey could not escape the attention of King Henry VIII and was seized during the Dissolution of the Monasteries around the year 1540. As brother-in-law to the King

(Herbert married Anne Parr, sister of Queen Consort Catherine Parr), William Herbert was granted the abbey and 46,000 acre estate in 1542. Eventually, Herbert was also granted the title of Earl of Pembroke, a tradition that continues today with the 18th Earl still a resident at Wilton House. Herbert's future was secured, and he began to enjoy the fruits of his labors at court by transforming his abandoned abbey into a fine, stately home.

The great Tudor mansion built by the first Earl of Pembroke lasted just eighty years, despite unsubstantiated rumors that the architect of the project was none other than Hans Holbein the Younger. Whether the artist was involved or not, the Gothic-renaissance entrance porch to the Tudor house was salvaged in the 19th century and is now known as the 'Holbein Porch.'

In the 1630s, the 4th Earl decided to demolish the southern wing of the house and erect several staterooms in its place. Using original designs said to have been drawn up by the famous Inigo Jones, the 4th Earl employed Jones' protégé Isaac de Caus to create a new south facade in a severe Palladian style. It has been discovered that the original plan was for two identical wings linked by a central portico, but the second wing was never built. Following a huge fire that ravaged Wilton House, Inigo Jones was enlisted, along with John Webb, to improve the house based on his original plan. The modifications carried out were considered a triumph.

The state rooms at Wilton House, designed by John Webb and Inigo Jones, are considered some of the finest and most lavishly decorated rooms in England. Designed to please the eye of royal guests, the staterooms are hung with a magnificent collection of paintings and filled with furniture by the greatest makers of the day.

Wilton's Colonnade Room was converted for a visit by King George III and features a rococo ceiling mural completed in the 1730s by Andien de Clermont. In the Great Ante-Room hangs one of Wilton's greatest treasures, a portrait of Rembrandt's mother painted by Rembrandt himself. The Single Cube Room introduces visitors to Jones' scheme of white plaster encrusted with gold, red walls, and pink carpets and features a painted canvas ceiling rendered by Italian painter Cavalier D'Arpino.

The Double Cube Room is considered the most stunning

room in the house. Around 60ft by 30ft by 30ft in size, this cavernous space was decorated to complement the van Dyck paintings that fill the wall panels and include a huge work depicting the 4th Earl and his family. The Corner Room, Little Ante Room, and The Hunting Room are the final three rooms created by Inigo Jones, Webb, and de Caus.

In 1705, the 8th Earl made some changes to Wilton House in order to accommodate his Arundel Marbles, but other than this minor intervention, Wilton remained largely unchanged until the 11th Earl took control in 1801. James Wyatt was enlisted by the 11th Earl to modernist Wilton House and provide more space for the Earl to display his growing collection of paintings and sculptures. Wyatt's architectural work at Wilton House was in the Gothic style, a change from his usual neoclassical approach.

The changes Wyatt made to the north front of the house, relocating an 'arc de triumph' from Wilton's park to the entrance forecourt and adding an equestrian statue of Marcus Aurelius, have not always been met with praise. However, Wyatt's addition of the cloisters, a two-storied gallery added in recognition of Wilton's monastic past, and the creation of a natural-light filled space to display the Pembroke collection of sculpture is largely celebrated.

A Palladian bridge by Roger Morris that sits astride the River Nadder is a highlight of Wilton's grounds and gardens. Wilton House has been open to the public since 1951, and since 2012, the 18th Earl, William Pembroke, has lived in the house with his family. Wilton House's 21 acres of landscaped parkland, particularly its water and rose gardens, are incredibly popular among visitors.

What Makes Wilton House Famous?

Wilton House has been described as being the best example of Palladian architecture in the UK; its Single and Double Cube Rooms have been described as being the finest staterooms in England, and its collection of van Dyck paintings has been described as the best in the world. The country seat of the Earls of Pembroke for over 400 years, Wilton House is an architectural and artistic gem.

Wilton House in TV and Film

- The Young Victoria (2009)
- Pride and Prejudice (2005)
- Mrs Brown (1997)
- Sense and Sensibility (1995)
- The Madness of King George (1994)
- The Bounty (1984)
- Blackadder (1986 TV Series)
- Barry Lyndon (1975)

Further Research

- Thomas Herbert Pembroke (2015) A Description of the Antiquities and Curiosities in Wilton House
- Neville Rodwell Wilkinson (2010) Wilton House Guide: A Handbook for Visitors.
- (1988) Wilton House and English Palladianism: Some Wiltshire Houses
- Sidney Herbert Pembroke (1968) A Catalogue of the paintings and drawings in the collection at Wilton House

Visitor Information

Wilton House is open to the public from April to August, Sundays to Thursdays. Opening hours are between 11:30 am and 5 pm, and admission charges are £14.50 for adults and £7.50 for children.

If traveling to Wilton House by train, get off at Salisbury Station. Buses R3 and R8 will take you from the station to Wilton House. If driving to Wilton House, head for Salisbury, just off the A36 for Warminster/Bath.

THE WARDOUR CASTLES
A Brief History of the Old and New Wardour Castle in Wiltshire

Key Facts about Wardour Castle

- Both Old and New Wardour Castle are located in the settlement of Wardour, part of Tisbury Parish in the county of Wiltshire, England.
- Old Wardour Castle was built in the late fourteenth century, and New Wardour Castle was completed in 1776.
- Old Wardour Castle is now a ruin managed by English Heritage, while New Wardour Castle is privately owned and was purchased in 2010 by designer Jaspar Conran.

In the fourteenth century, Baron Lovell returned triumphant from battles overseas and built Wardour Castle, a grand fortress worthy of a powerful English Lord. Originally built as a show of strength and victory over enemies overseas, Wardour Castle was eventually ruined by enemies on home soil after being besieged in both the Wars of the Roses and the English Civil Wars. In the 18th century, the owners of the decaying castle decided to save the charming ruin and build a new castle, actually a neoclassical country house, just over a mile away. The ruin was kept as a romantic garden decoration.

Following his experiences fighting in France during the Hundred Years War, Lord Lovel of Titchmarsh returned to England with the desire to build a grand fortress in the style of a fourteenth-century French chateau. Lord Lovel was granted permission from King Richard II in 1392 and immediately set about designing a stronghold worthy of a powerful English lord. Master mason William Wynford was in charge of the building of Old Wardour Castle and used local Tisbury greensand as his primary material, a green sandstone rock local to the area. The six-sided, hexagonal design of the castle is unique in Britain, and its several self-contained guest suites are the only ones of their kind that date back to the 14th century.

Originally, the castle's front door was protected by a wide ditch with a drawbridge, portcullis, and projecting barbican that would have been used to defend the front entrance. Above the portal, over the front entrance, the Arundell coat-of-arms can be seen, presided over by a depiction of the head of Christ. The central courtyard at Old Wardour Castle would have originally been in the shape of a hexagon with four or five stories built up on every side, and there is evidence of an old well in the courtyard that is thought to have been sheltered by an elaborate roof, delicately painted with the emblems of the Lovell family.

The Lovell family did not stay in favor of the crown for long as Francis Lovell, the 9th Baron Lovell, supported the losing side in the War of the Roses. The 9th Baron's open support of doomed Richard III meant Old Wardour Castle was confiscated from him in 1461. After passing through the hands of a few different owners, Old Wardour Castle was purchased and again confiscated, this time from the Arundell family, an ancient Cornish clan with a prominent position in English society. Sir Thomas Arundell, a Roman Catholic, was executed for treason in 1552 during the turbulent reign of Edward VI.

The Arundell family bought Old Wardour Castle back in 1570, but things didn't get much better for the persecuted family when the English Civil War broke out. As Catholic landowners, the Arundell's supported the crown. In 1643, Thomas Arundell, 2nd Baron Arundell of Wardour, left to fight for the King, leaving his wife, Lady Blanche Arundell, and just 25 fighting men to defend the castle. Sir Edward Hungerford stormed the castle with 1,300 Parliamentarian men and laid siege for five days straight. Lady Arundell surrendered only after it became clear that the castle was threatened with complete destruction and Colonel Edmund

Ludlow took control.

Lord Arundell died of his wounds at the Battle of Landsdowne, but the Royalists would not accept such a defeat and laid siege to the castle for ten months. Led by Lord Arundell's son, Henry 3rd Lord Arundell, Old Wardour Castle was heavily bombed, and its outer walls were destroyed. On March 18th, 1644, the castle was surrendered.

The Arundells were able to return to the ruined castle in the 1680s, but it wasn't until the 8th Baron took control of Old Wardour Castle that the family was able to borrow sufficient funds to begin rebuilding it. Rather than trying to salvage what remained of the besieged castle and build a country house from the rubble up, the 8th Baron decided to start from scratch on a patch of land approximately 1.5 miles away, retaining the ruined castle as a romantic focal point within the new castle grounds.

In the year 1769, building began on the New Wardour Castle, designed by architect James Paine, known for his distinctive Palladian style. It took over seven years to build the castle, which is not really a castle at all but a neoclassical country house. Characteristic of

18th-century design, New Wardour Castle features a square main block flanked by symmetrical pavilions and is constructed from limestone ashlar. The most noteworthy feature of New Wardour Castle is its rotunda staircase, which measures 144 feet across. The ground floor in this part of the house is made from impressive black and white marble, while the floors of the next level of the house are made from wood and feature typically neoclassical Roman columns rising to a vaulted dome ceiling decorated with reliefs of musical instruments.

The Roman Catholic chapel at New Wardour Castle still holds Sunday services for the local community. Known as All Saints Chapel, the chapel is Grade I listed and is also used for musical events. The gardens at New Wardour Castle were drawn up by George Ingham in 1773 and further modified by Capability Brown between 1775 and 1783. Today, the gardens feature a walled garden with a swimming pool, a temple garden, and a Camellia House.

The 16th and last Lord Arundell of Wardour died in 1944, leaving New Wardour Castle up for rent. A public school took over the lease and modified the building to accommodate classrooms, dormitories, and a dining room. After more than fifty years in residence, the school closed, and New Wardour Castle was sold for less than £1 million to property developer Nigel Tuersley, who converted it into ten luxury apartments. In the year 2010, designer Jaspar Conran bought the English Heritage Grade I listed New Wardour House and is thought to have lived there for part of the year.

What Makes Wardour Castle Famous?

Old Wardour Castle was the first hexagonally-shaped castle in England, inspired by the great chateaus of fourteenth-century France, and is famous for being confiscated by Henry VIII and stormed and captured by Parliamentarian forces during the English Civil War. In contemporary times, both Old Wardour and New Wardour Castle have been used as locations in hit films. Old Wardour Castle is featured heavily in Robin Hood: Prince of Thieves, and New Wardour Castle is featured in Billy Elliot.

Anglotopia's Take

This is our 'local' castle when we stay nearby in Dorset. It's a romantic, iconic ruin, well worth seeing, especially for 90s kids who grew up with Kevin Costner's Robin Hood film. But there's so much more to the place. It's a ruin, and if you go off-season, you'll often have the place to yourself. It's quite fun to explore all the nooks, crannies, and staircases that go nowhere. There's also a lovely walk that takes in the wider Wardour estate, and it's worth the short walk over to 'New' Wardour Castle to see the beautiful (and private) Palladian home and grounds. It's been divided up into flats and besides a small chapel, pretty much never open to the public. But it's worth admiring from the outside. And as it's private homes now, it's very quiet, and you almost feel like you're trespassing (you're not as long as you stick to the public footpath). It is quite remote - even when you're local, it takes quite a circuitous route on narrow country lanes to get there. You can pretty much only get there by car.

Wardour Castle in TV and Film

Old Wardour Castle

- Robin Hood: Prince of Thieves (1991)
- Chronos (1985 Documentary)
- The Stately Ghosts of England (1965 TV Movie)

New Wardour Castle

- Billy Elliot (2000)
- Four Seasons (2008 Mini-Series)

Further Research

- Mark Giroud (2012) Old Wardour Castle

- Barry Williamson (2011) The Arundells of Wardour

Visitor Information

Old Wardour Castle is maintained by English Heritage and is open to the public daily during the summer months. Entry is free to English Heritage members, but a small fee applies to non-members. For full opening times and price list, see the English Heritage website. New Wardour Castle is not open to the public, but the grounds are open to public footpaths (there is a Catholic chapel inside the house that is occasionally open to the public).

The nearest train station to both Old and New Wardour Castle is Tisbury, 3 ½ miles away. A local bus service, No 26, will take you from the train station to the castle. If traveling by car, Old and New Wardour Castles are located off the A30 road, 3 ½ miles southwest of Tisbury.

KEDLESTON HALL
The Temple of the Arts in Derbyshire

Key Facts about Kedleston Hall

- Kedleston Hall is located in Kedleston, Derbyshire, four miles from Derby.
- The present Kedleston Hall was built in 1759 by Sir Nathanial Curzon.
- Kedleston Hall has been in the Curzon family since it was built. Although the property is now owned by the National Trust, the current Curzon family continues to live there.

The partnership of the wealthy and esteemed 5th Baronet Sir Nathanial Curzon and innovative architect Robert Adam was always going to result in something spectacular. In 1758, on the occasion of his inheritance, Curzon set out to build an elegant house in the height of fashion, sparing no expense. Robert Adam made his dreams come true, creating in Kedleston Hall a neoclassical masterpiece so unrivaled in its lavish interiors it came to be known as the Temple of the Arts.

The Curzon family came to England with the Norman Conquest and owned the estate of Kedleston from the late 13th century. The inheritance that came to Sir Nathanial Curzon in 1758 was substantial, and he immediately hired respected Palladian architects James Paine and Matthew Brettingham to design a new house. Brettingham and Paine set out to make Curzon's dreams of outdoing his Tory peers at Chatsworth come true, successfully building Kedleston's two-wing houses in 1759, but as they began work on the main house, to their dismay, Curzon met Robert Adam.

Robert Adam had recently returned from the Mediterranean and was completing some minor designs for garden temples to improve the landscape of Kedleston's park. These humble designs were enough to impress Curzon, and he hired Adams to take over the entire project of Kedleston Hall.

The Palladian front created by the previous architects was retained, but Adams constructed a facade of his own to the rear of the mansion. The Robert Adam exterior is based on the Arch of Constantine in Rome and features a large, centrally placed glass door with a pediment above that is connected to the ground floor by two staircases, curving gracefully down to the garden. The house consisted of three blocks: the central contained the state rooms and was intended only for the use of important guests, the east was a complete house on its own and where the family resided, and the west contained the kitchens and servants' quarters.

Curzon's original plan to add two further quadrants to the three that made up Kedleston Hall never came to fruition, so Adams' impact on the exterior of Kedleston Hall remained limited to his magnificent south facade. The interiors, however, are another matter. In Kedleston's interiors, Adams created a monument to the glories of ancient Rome. Channeling the aesthetics of the Roman Empire itself, Adams' designs were inspired by Emperor Diocletian's palace in Split and are a perfectly preserved example of the Georgian's mania for classical extravagance.

The glass door on the south facade leads directly into the Marble Hall, the walls of which are lined with 20 columns of Derbyshire marble and adorned with statues and relief panels showing scenes from classical antiquity. The floor is inlaid with Italian marble. The adjoining saloon, like the marble hall, rises to the full height of the house and is lit by natural daylight through a glass oculus in the ceiling. Based on the Pantheon, this circular chamber was designed as a sculpture gallery and features intricate ceiling rosettes, heavy pediments, and scagliola columns on each of the doorways.

The state apartments are most notable for their fine furniture and paintings, while the dining room wows with its ceiling based on the Palace of Augustus. In the rooms on the lower level where the family lived, you can see Lord Curzon's Eastern Museum. A treasure trove of curiosities, Kedleston's resident museum contains a collection of Far Eastern artifacts amassed by Lord Curzon during his time as Viceroy of India at the beginning of the 20th century. Lady Curzon's Delhi Durbah Coronation dress of 1903, known as the Peacock Dress, is the most celebrated and dazzling piece in the collection.

Unusually, the grounds at Kedleston Hall were also designed by Robert Adam. Adam favored a natural-looking landscape but completed designs for buildings on the grounds that would rival many stately homes in their scale and intricacy. The only structures to make it past the design stage were the fishing lodge, bridge, and cascade. In later years, a summerhouse and orangery were added, but for the most part, the gardens and grounds remain just as they were over 200 years ago.

In 1939, Richard Curzon, 2nd Viscount Scarsdale, offered Keddleston Hall for use by the UK War Department, and in 1986, the owners of Kedleston Hall passed on the mansion, known by some as the Temple of Arts, in pristine condition, to the National Trust.

Why is Kedleston Hall Famous?

Known as the Temple of Arts, Kedleston Hall is famous as much for its rooms as what can be found inside the rooms. One of the best-surviving examples of Robert Adam's flamboyant architectural style and Ancient Rome-inspired interiors, Kedleston Hall is a snapshot of 18th-century Britain's obsession with all things neoclassical. West meets East at Kedleston Hall, which is also home to Lord Curzon's Eastern Museum, a collection of artifacts amassed by the Lord during his time as Viceroy of India.

Kedleston Hall in TV and Film

- Tarzan (2016)
- The Duchess (2008)

- Jane Eyre (2006 mini-series)
- War and Peace (1972 mini-series)
- Women in Love (1969)

Further Research

- Roy Adams (2010) Tiaras and Tantrums: 25 Years of Service at Kedleston Hall
- National trust (1999) Kedleston Hall
- Leslie Harris and Gervase Jackson-Stops (1987) Robert Adam and Kedleston: The Making of a Neoclassical Masterpiece

Visitor Information

Kedleston Hall is run by the National Trust and is open to the public every day except Fridays, from 12 until 5 pm during the summer months. From October to April, the house is closed, but the ground and gardens remain open to the public. Admission charges are currently £10.50 for adults and £5.30 for adults. For more information on opening hours and prices, see the website, www.nationaltrust.org/kedleston-hall.

To access Kedleston Hall by train, go to Duffield Station, which is 3 ½ miles from the property, or Derby Station, which is 5 ½ miles away. By car, from Derby, follow the A38 north, take the first exit, and continue along Kedleston Road, following the brown tourist signs.

FORDE ABBEY
A Former Monastery Turned Stately Home in Dorset

Key Facts about Forde Abbey

- Forde Abbey is located in Dorset, England (but has a Somerset Address).
- The original abbey was built between 1141 and 1148 and was used as a Cistercian monastery for almost 400 years.
- Forde Abbey was surrendered to the crown in 1539 and remains in private ownership to this day.

Forde Abbey has provided a home to Cistercian Monks, one of Oliver Cromwell's top Parliamentarian aides, a penny-pinching Victorian merchant, and finally, an enterprising 21st-century family who transformed it into a working estate and tourist attraction. Standing among the stunning scenery of West Dorset for over 850 years, the Abbey is the perfect example of a pre-Reformation monastery turned into a late Renaissance palace and reborn as a tourist attraction and working estate.

Forde Abbey has existed under many guises. Built early in the 12th century as a Cistercian monastic house, the Abbey was originally home to just twelve monks. By the sixteenth century, Forde Abbey had become renowned as one of England's great seats of learning and increased dramatically in size, wealth, and grandiosity until it reached its apex under the last abbot of Forde, Thomas Chard.

Under Abbot Chard, Forde Abbey's Great Hall and Entrance Tower were said to be so lavishly and decadently ornamented that it was only a matter of time before the monastery caught the attention of the Crown. In 1539, with King Henry VIII's Dissolution of the Monasteries well underway, Abbot Chard surrendered Forde Abbey peacefully to the Crown.

Sadly, Forde Abbey's next incarnation was that of a forgotten relic. This once-thriving monastery became derelict and was plundered for its valuable stone by a succession of absentee landlords for the next hundred years. Then, in 1649, Forde Abbey was purchased by Edmund Prideaux, who saw promise in the Abbey's private residences and sweeping grounds and set about transforming it from a monastic residence into a private home.

Edmund Prideaux was a strong supporter of the Parliamentary cause and, as well as being a Member of Parliament and Treasurer of the Inner Temple, he became Cromwell's attorney-general for most of the Interregnum. Prideaux's position as one of Cromwell's top aides was a lucrative one, and his transformation of the Abbey into his personal mansion was an extravagant affair.

Puritan values by the wayside, Prideaux added a west wing to the existing monastery and added a grand fireplace and staircase to the Forde Abbey's Great Hall. The stairs to Prideaux's staterooms feature carved wooden flower urns, a Spanish balustrade, and a particularly intricately plastered ceiling. The Grand Saloon is home to the famous Mortlake tapestries. Based on the cartoons by Raphael held by the V&A, the tapestries were made in 1620 and were once confiscated from Forde Abbey by Judge Jeffreys but returned by Queen Anne.

The rooms now known as the Prideaux Rooms were added to Forde Abbey as part of a reception suite to the salon and include bedrooms and dressing rooms, all featuring his impressive ceilings. One of these rooms features a four-poster bed with a red damask canopy made for Queen Anne, who never got to enjoy her planned visit to the abbey in 1714 as she died earlier that year.

Although the work of Prideaux and his architect Edward Carter dominate Forde Abbey, some parts of the original monastery do remain. Unfortunately, the abbey church was demolished after the dissolution, but the structure of the Great Hall was saved and now houses two religious statues, the only surviving artifacts of the original church. Prideaux converted the Chapter House into a chapel by installing a carved oak screen and a pulpit. Members of the Prideaux and Gwyn family are buried in the crypt below.

The former monks' dormitory has been preserved, as has the north side of the Old Cloisters, which was refaced and ornamented by Abbot Chard in a virtuoso Gothic style. The Upper Refectory is a favorite among visitors. Previously, the space was allotted to meat-eating monks who were required to dine separately from their vegetarian colleagues. A minstrel gallery was installed by Prideaux, and the area is now a library.

Like many great houses, Forde Abbey was saved from unsympathetic renovations during the 18th and 19th centuries thanks to the financial ruin of its owners. Following Prideaux's death in 1659, Forde Abbey passed to his son, also Edmund Prideaux. Under the pretext of having entertained the doomed Duke of Monmouth, Prideaux was accused of supporting Monmouth's rebellion against James II. Arrested, imprisoned, and ruined, Prideaux retained possession of Forde Abbey and passed down through the lineage of his family but with little alteration or repair apart from the creation of its magnificent gardens.

Unable to afford the upkeep of Forde Abbey, Prideaux's descendants rented the house to philosopher Jeremy Bentham, who turned it into a meeting place for some of the greatest thinkers of the early 19th century. During the Victorian years, the house again entered a spell of massive decline when it was sold, including all of its lands and contents, to a merchant named Miles, who appeared to live in just five rooms and left the rest of the house to rot.

In the late 19th century, Forde Abbey entered the possession of the Evans family, who made huge investments into repair and restoration and passed the house on to the Ropers, who own it today. In the 1970s, the owners of Forde Abbey modernized the house and developed cattle farming and soft fruit growing orchards on the estate. Today, Forde Abbey is a family home, working estate, and popular Dorset tourist attraction.

What Makes Forde Abbey Famous?

Forde Abbey is truly beautiful, and today, its 30 acres of gardens are one of its main attractions. Now a private home, Forde Abbey is the perfect example of a monastery that survived Henry VIII's dissolution of the monasteries, was transformed into a grand stately home, and, through a mixture of nurture and neglect, survived to this day for the general public to enjoy. Home to the renowned Mortlake tapestries and England's tallest powered fountain, Forde Abbey is one of Dorset's many historic treasures.

Forde Abbey in TV and Film

- Far from the Madding Crowd (2015)
- Daniel Deronda (2002 mini-series)
- Restoration (1995)

Further Research

- Stephen Friar (2010) Cathedrals and Abbeys
- John Roper (1968) Forde Abbey
- Forde Abbey Trust (2003) Forde Abbey and Gardens: 850 Years of History

Visitor Information

Forde Abbey Gardens are open to the public all year round, but Forde Abbey House is only open from April until the end of October each year, Tuesdays to Sundays. For more information on opening times and prices, please see the website, www.fordeabbey.co.uk.

Forde Abbey is not very accessible by public transport, but there are various walking and cycling trails available for the larger West Dorset area. If driving, use the M5 and leave the motorway at Junction 25 for Taunton. Take the A358 to Chard. If traveling from Exeter, take the A30 to Honiton, the A35 to Axminster, then the

A358 to Chard.

THE GREENWAY ESTATE
The Home of Agatha Christie

Key Facts about the House

- The Greenway Estate is located on the River Dart near Galmpton in Devon.
- Greenway House was built in the late 18th century by Roope Harris Roope.
- Novelist Agatha Christie and her husband have owned the Greenway Estate since 1938.

Around the 1920s, during the golden age of detective fiction, the English Country House became a crime scene. In 1938, the Queen of Crime herself, Agatha Christie, bought a crime scene of her very own with the purchase of the Greenway Estate in which she lived and worked for the remainder of her life. This huge Georgian house is now owned by the National Trust and is a bricks-and-mortar monument to Christie's magnificent legacy in ink and paper.

The first property to be built on the Greenway Estate was a Tudor mansion erected in the 16th century by the Gilbert family. Humphrey Gilbert, a soldier during the reign of Elizabeth I and Member of Parliament, was born here, but little else is known about this first Tudor house. We do know that the current Greenway House was built in the late 18th century by a man named Roope Harris Roope and was altered and added to by subsequent owners until it was purchased by Agatha Christie and her husband Max Mallowan in 1938.

Agatha Christie is said to have grown up admiring Greenway from her home in Torquay. When the property came up for sale at the price of £6,000, she convinced her husband that they should buy it, and it became their holiday home. Visitors to Greenway can wander through the Mallowan family's drawing room, which is furnished with historical items from Christie's childhood home in Torquay, the kitchen, still kitted out with 20th-century appliances, and the sitting room, full of objects acquired on Max's many archaeological digs.

Just a few of the treasures on display in Greenway House include the Damascus Chest, a beautifully hand-crafted chest purchased by Max Mallowan that resides in the couple's bedroom, a Steinway piano that Christie is said to have been too shy to play despite being a concert-level pianist and the world's second mobile phone, purchased by Anthony Hicks for use when he was working in the gardens.

As well as a large country house, the Greenway Estate contained a tennis court, planted with an impressive magnolia campbellii by Max Mallowan in 1938, a kitchen garden, vinery, and bird pond, featuring a sculpture by Bridget McCrum, as well as numerous beautifully planted gardens around the house. The driveway was laid in the 1820s in a sweeping Reptonian style.

Greenway Estate and its surroundings are often featured in Agatha Christie's novels. In the novel Five Little Pigs, completed in 1942, Christie uses the footpath leading from the main house to the battery overlooking the River Dart as a key location in the inevitable murder. In Towards Zero (1944), the river again features as a convenient geographical feature for one of the suspects who disappears each night for a swim, and in Dead Man's Folly (1956), the boat house of Greenway House is the place where the first murder victim is discovered.

The boathouse at Greenway is referred to as 'Raleigh's Boathouse' due to an incident involving Sir Walter Raleigh, a pipe, and a fire-fighting servant with a pint of ale. Raleigh's Boathouse is thought to date back to late Georgian times and features a plunge pool directly into the river, a sunbathing salon, and a balcony with a fireplace.

When Christie died in 1976, Greenway was occupied by her husband, Max Mallowan, until he died in 1978. Their daughter Rosalind Hicks and her husband lived in the house until Rosalind's death in 2004, at which point the estate was acquired by the National Trust. Now a Grade II listed building, Greenway House, its gardens and accompanying art gallery are open to the public. During the winter months, the house closes to the public, so the National Trust's team of conservators can condition check, clean, and pack away the many important objects in the house's collection.

Featured in TV and Film

- Agatha Christie's Poirot, Dead Man's Folly (2013) TV Series
- Being Poirot (2013) Documentary

Further Research

- Jackie Bennet and Richard Hanson (2014) The Writer's Garden: How Garden's Inspired our Best-Loved Authors
- Mathew Prichard and Hilary Macaskill (2014) Agatha Christie at Home
- National Trust (2010) Greenway, Devon.
- Laura Thompson (2008) Agatha Christie: An English Mystery
- Agatha Christie (2001) An Autobiography
- Agatha Christie (1956) Dead Man's Folly
- Agatha Christie (1944) Towards Zero
- Agatha Christie (1942) Three Little Pigs

Visiting Information

Greenway Estates are open to the public between the months of March and October between the hours of 10.30 am and 5 pm. Entry costs £9.90 for adults and £4.95 for children. The closest airport to Greenway is Exeter International Airport, which is approximately 50 miles away.

Suppose traveling to Greenway by car from Torbay follows signs to Brixham until you reach the village of Churston. Follow brown tourist signs right through the village of Galmpton until you reach Greenway, which has a postcode of TQ5 0ES. Greenway is accessible by train from the nearby towns of Paignton and Churston. From Paignton, you can travel to Greenway by steam train, but the station is 30 30-minute walk from the Greenway estate. A vintage bus service is available every day from Torquay, Paignton, and Brixham to Greenway. You can also use a park-and-ride ferry service from Dartmouth to Greenway, which includes a quay car shuttle service from the quay to the property reception, or arrange to bring your own boat!

    For more detailed information, visit the website www.nationaltrust.org.uk/greenway.

SUDELEY CASTLE
A Classic House That Played a Role Throughout British History

Key Facts about the House

- Sudeley Castle is located in near Winchcombe in the Cotswolds, Gloucestershire, England.
- Sudeley Castle was built in 1442 by Ralph Boteler, Baron of Sudeley. There may have been a castle on the site since the 12th
- The castle was owned by the Duke of Gloucester, who later became King Richard III, Edward VI, and Thomas Seymour, who was married to the dowager Queen Catherine Parr.

Like every good medieval palace, Sudeley Castle has played host to many of the most notorious royals, influential politicians, and aristocratic families of English History. Sudeley Castle is linked to not one but two of Henry VIII's wives and has been owned by the crown at various times. Saved by new money, Sudeley Castle became the antiquarian palace it is today at the hands of a certain Mrs Emma Dent, a Victorian historian and eccentric who made the castle into her own private kingdom.

The original owner and founder of Sudelely Castle, Saxon lord Ralph Boteler, managed to build the sizable castle, gardens, and chapel with money he made during the Hundred Year's War. The Botelers weren't as fortunate during the War of the Roses, however, as Sudeley Castle was too important a stronghold to be left in peace. In 1469, King Edward IV of England confiscated the castle and gave it to the Duke of Gloucester, later Richard III of England.

The next hundred years were a tumultuous time for Sudeley

as the castle was first used by Richard as a base for the Battle of Tewkesbury. After Richard became King, he built the banqueting hall and royal suite but did not live to enjoy them as he was killed at the Battle of Bosworth. Sudeley passed to Henry VII, who passed it to his uncle, the Duke of Bedford. On Henry VIII's succession, Sudeley once again belonged to the crown.

The next period of Sudeley's history is its most romantic and tragic. Thomas Seymour, who was said to be a handsome but reckless man, proposed to virgin Queen Elizabeth I before taking the hand of Catherine Parr, widower of Henry VIII and stepmother to Elizabeth. Sudeley Castle became the newlywed's honeymoon palace, with Thomas insisting on rebuilding the castle in accordance with his new wife's royal status. Soon, Queen Catherine was pregnant, and it was decided that she would live at Sudeley for the final months of her pregnancy. Accompanied by Lady Jane Grey, her sister Lady Pembroke, and over 100 other ladies and gentlemen of the household, Catherine gave birth to Lady Mary Seymour on 30th August 1548. Unfortunately, Catherine died just five days after the birth, and soon after, Lord Seymour was executed for treason after reportedly plotting against Protector Somerset, guardian of the boy King Edward VI.

During the English Civil War, Sudeley and its owners again fared badly, as Lord Chandos declared for the king, leaving the castle mostly destroyed by parliamentarians and in ruins for almost two centuries. It is here that we welcome to the stage the Victorians, in particular the Dent brothers, who made their fortune with a glove-making business in Worcestershire and acquired Sudeley Castle in 1837, the same year as Queen Victoria's ascension to the throne. The brothers immediately hired Sir Gilbert Scott, who stabilized the ruins and rebuilt and restored the north quadrangle and south court. Scott's work retained as much of the medieval spirit of the castle as possible, adding spectacular Gothic furnishings and fittings, many bought from Horace Walpole's Strawberry Hill in London.

The Dent brothers passed Sudeley on to their nephew John Dent and his wife Emma, whose reign at Sudeley gave it the quirky Victorian character it has retained to this day. Emma Dent was a historian and collector who corresponded with some of the greatest minds and most famous celebrities of the 19th century. The most pleasing room at Sudelely Castle is the library, which features a 16th-century fireplace and a gorgeous Elizabethan tapestry. The bedroom suite, too, is spectacular and was designed and furnished by William Morris. Sudeley Castle has nine gardens, the centerpiece of which is the Queen's Garden, named after the four English Queens, Catherine Parr, Lady Jane Seymour, Elizabeth I, and Anne Boleyn, who are said to have admired it.

Sudely Castle is still privately owned but is open to the public as a tourist attraction. Current owner Elizabeth, Lady Ashcombe, and her late husband Henry Cubitt, 4th Baron of Ashcombe, made major renovations to the castle in 1969 in order to open it up to the public. Lady Ashcombe and her children, Henry and Mollie, now manage Sudeley Castle as a visitor attraction.

What Makes Sudeley Castle Famous?

Sudeley Castle was a military stronghold and royal residence much fought over during medieval times. This rich history, combined with the eye for interiors and eccentric lifestyle of its Victorian owners, has made Sudeley one of the most fascinating private residences in England. Sudeley Castle is also said to be haunted by Queen Dowager Catherine Parr. Following her sudden death in 1548, Catherine's body was buried in the grounds of Sudeley Castle, only to disappear during the civil war. Her coffin was rediscovered by a local man in 1782, opened and reburied only for it to be re-opened and her body re-buried, upside down, in 1792. Eventually, Catherine's body was laid to rest in the tomb of Lord Chandos in St Mary's chapel. Sightings of Catherine's ghost, in green Tudor attire, are reported to this day.

Featured in TV and Film

- Father Brown (2013) Tv Series
- Tess of the D'Urbervilles (2008) mini-series
- Elizabeth (2000) TV documentary

- Emma (1996) TV movie
- Castle Ghosts of England (1995) TV Series

Further Research

- Lady Ashcombe (2009) Behind Castle Walls at Sudeley Past and Present
- Nicholas Hart (1994) Sudeley Castle and Gardens
- Alison Weir (2007) The Six Wives of Henry VIII

Visiting Information

Sudeley Castle and Gardens are open to the public between March and October each year. An all-day adult pass costs £14, and a child pass costs £5.

Sudeley Castle is just 71km from Birmingham Airport, 74km from Coventry Airport, and 98km from Bristol Airport. If traveling by car, use the postcode GL54 5JD. Sudeley Castle is 10 miles from Junction 9 of the M5, 43 miles from the M4, and 61 miles from the M40 motorway at Oxford. The closest train station to Sudeley Castle is Cheltenham Spa. A bus service operates between Winchcombe and Cheltenham or Broadway.

For more detailed travel information, see the website www.sudeleycastle.co.uk

DUNHAM MASSEY
A Georgian Masterpiece Near Manchester

Key Facts about Dunham Massey

- Dunham Massey House is located in Dunham Town, Greater Manchester, England.
- The current house was built in 1616 by Sir George Booth.
- Dunham Massey House is currently part-owned by the National Trust, with members of the Stamford family living in it as National Trust tenants.

As with many of the great houses of England, it is not the bricks and mortar of Dunham Massey that makes it exceptional, but its complex and multi-layered family history. A largely Georgian house built by the 2nd Earl of Warrington, Dunham Massey, has survived as a place of great wealth and bankruptcy for the last 300 years remaining, against the odds, in the possession of the same family who built it.

The civil parish of Dunham Massey was owned by the Massey family from the early 13th century until the line became extinct in 1409. A castle existed in Dunham Massey but was demolished by the Elizabethan period, and Dunham Massey Hall, home of the manorial lord, was demolished in 1616, making way for Sir George Booth to build the current Dunham Massey House.

Sir George Booth was made a baronet by James I in 1611, but even the favor of the King cannot guarantee prosperity, and Booth died at the age of 42 with huge debts that passed down to his son and inheritor George Booth, 2nd Earl of Warrington. Learning a lesson in financial management from his reckless father, the 2nd Earl married for money and married the daughter of a London merchant for her £40,000 dowry. The 2nd Earl used his unfortunate wife's money to rebuild Dunham Massey, and between the years of 1732 and 1740, John Norris was employed to transform the house into a grand Georgian mansion.

The 2nd Earl and his wife had one child, a daughter, and then lived apart for the rest of their days. This daughter married Harry Grey, 4th Earl of Stamford, and the house passed happily down the generations until it reached the 7th Earl, who is said to have married a woman who performed in the circus. The 7th Earl gambled the family's fortune and fled Dunham Massey, leaving the mansion uninhabited.

The lives of successive owners of Dunham Massey were no less extraordinary. The title passed next to a clergyman in South Africa who was married to an indigenous Khoikhoi woman. Their son, John, lay claim to Dunham Massey on his father's death and was bought off by the property's trustees.

The next and 9th Earl was also a man of the cloth, a clergyman from Canada whose liberal politics passed down to his son, who took over the earldom when the 9th Earl died just three years later. Dunham Massey entered a brief but important period of its history during the Great War when it was offered by the 9th Earl's widow, Penelope, for use as an auxiliary hospital from April 1917 to January 1919. The hospital, known as Stamford Military Hospital, has recently been recreated within Dunham Massey as part of a centenary commemoration of The Great War.

Once old enough, Penelope's son, the 10th Earl, took control of Dunham Massey. An active peer, the 10th Earl supported the United Nations and invited Haile Selassie, Emperor of Ethiopia and messianic leader of the Rastafarian movement, to stay at Dunham Massey in 1938, a visit that led to a lifelong friendship. The 10th Earl never married and passed the property on to the National Trust on his death in 1976.

Visitors to Dunham Massey will enter through the entrance hall in the South front. Lady Stamford's parlor to the right has been left exactly as it was on her departure in 1959. The saloon, created during Georgian renovations, is now furnished as an Edwardian drawing room and features Stamford family portraits by Romney. The Great Hall features plasterwork by Inigo Jones, and the Great Gallery is hung with a grand topographical study of the Dunham Massey estate through time. Also in the gallery is a significant painting by Guernico, An Allegory of Time. Grinling Gibbon's early carving, The Crucifixion hangs over the mantelpiece in the library while other treasures dotted around the house include a collection of Huguenot silver and an antique bust of Emperor Hadrian, probably acquired by the 5th Earl.

Why is Dunham Massey Famous?

Dunham Massey is the only surviving medieval park in Trafford and enjoys up to 200,000 visits from the public each year. The house has not only survived for over three centuries but has remained in the same family throughout this time, each descendent of George Booth, 1st Earl of Warrington, completely unique in character and lifestyle. It was visited once by Haile Selassie and almost lost thanks to the 7th Earl, who quite literally ran away with the circus; Dunham Massey has many stories to tell.

Featured in TV and Film

- Secrets of the Manor House (2012) TV Series
- The Memoirs of Sherlock Holmes (1994) TV Series
- The Casebook of Sherlock Holmes (1991) TV series
- The Return of Sherlock Holmes (1986) TV Series

Further Research

- National Trust (2000) Dunham Massey
- Pamela Sambrook (1999) A Country House at Work: Three Centuries of Dunham Massey
- James Lomax (2006) Country House Silver at Dunham Massey

- David Eastwood (2004) The Booths of Dunham Massey

Visiting Information

Dunham Massey is open to the public between March and October every day apart from Thursday and Friday between the hours of 11 am and 5 pm. The nearest airport to Dunham Massey is Manchester Airport, and the postcode is WA14 4SJ. If traveling to Dunham Massey by car, take Exit 19 from the M6 or Exit 7 from the M56. Trains are available from nearby Altrincham and Hale, and buses are available from Altrincham and Warrington.

Visit the website www.nationaltrust.org.uk/dunham-massey for more detailed information.

Image © By Matt Ellery

POLESDEN LACEY
Where the Queen Mother Spent Her Honeymoon

Key Facts about Polesden Lacey

- The first house to be built on the site of Polesden Lacey was erected in 1336. The word 'polesden' is thought to be Saxon in origin.
- The estate was bought by William McEwan in 1906 for his daughter and her husband, Captain the Honorable Ronald Greville.
- Polesden Lacey was bequeathed to the National Trust in 1942 by Mrs Margaret Greville.

Polesden Lacey's fame comes not so much from the triumph of its architecture or the lure of its sumptuous Edwardian interiors but from its most notorious owner, Mrs Greville, whose entertaining of the stars of English society was legendary. The existing Regency house located in Surrey, England, was completely rebuilt by Mrs Greville in 1906 with the main objective of creating a space fit to entertain kings and Queens. To Mrs Greville's undoubted joy, King George VI and Queen Elizabeth spent part of their honeymoon here in 1923.

The first medieval house built on the site of Polesden Lacey was purchased and rebuilt by Anthony Rous in 1630. The next known owner is the famous Georgian poet and playwright Richard Brinsley Sheridan, who bought the house in 1804 only for it to be demolished in 1824 by Joseph Bronsor and completely rebuilt by Thomas Cubit, builder of Belgravia. The estate was next sold to the fabulously named Sir Walter Rockcliff Farquhar. At Farquhar's death in 1902, the house passed briefly into the hands of civil servant Sir

Clinton Edward Dawkins before being bought by William McEwan.

It is now, in 1906, that Polesden Lacey is finally able to throw open its doors and stretch out its wings, coming to life in a blitz of opulent and intimate socializing that is said to have drawn in Prime Ministers, celebrities, and heads of state from all over the world. But first, Polesden had to transform itself into a lavish setting fit for the sort of exclusive soirees Mrs Greville had planned.

Mrs Greville was heir to a sizeable fortune amassed by her father, William McEwan, founder and owner of the Scottish McEwan brewery company. On the purchase of the house, Mrs Greville employed architects Mewes and Davis, famous for their design of the Ritz hotels to convert the interiors of Polesden Lacey to reflect her social standing.

The exterior of the house, which dates to Cubitt's rebuilding of 1821, is neo-classical in design, with the look of a seaside villa perched on the edge of a steep slope and surrounded by a sizeable park. The interiors of the house are pure Edwardian decadence. The drawing room is an ornately carved masterpiece in gilt, mirror, and velvet, while the great dining room boasts a collection of paintings that are amongst the National Trust's finest treasures, including portraits by British artists Raeburn, Lawrence, and Reynolds. In the barrel-vaulted Jacobean corridor, there hangs work by de Hooch and van Goyen as well as a larger-than-life portrait of Mrs Greville herself by Carolus-Duran. An astonishing collection of furniture, silver, porcelain, and paintings adorn each reception room and gallery at Polesden Lacey, and the library is lovely, as is Mrs Greville's study, which contains a collection of Meissen and Furstenberg oriental tea caddies.

Unfortunately, Mr Ronald Greville didn't live to enjoy the magnificence of his new home, as he died just two years after the purchase of Polesden Lacey. Rather than entering a period of protracted private and public mourning as Queen Victoria did over fifty years later, Margaret Greville's social activity increased, and over the next 30 years, she became one of the most celebrated hostesses of the times. In 1923, George VI and Queen Elizabeth accepted Margaret's invitation to spend their honeymoon at Polesden Lacey, securing the house's favorable place in the imagination of the

British public with a large newspaper feature article complete with photographs.

Polesden Lacey has belonged to the National Trust since 1942 and, in 1995, was extensively restored. In 2012-2013, Polesden Lacey's visitor figures made it one of the top ten most visited National Trust sites. Originally, it was thought that some areas of the house, namely the Servants' quarters, were not of interest to the public, and so were used by National Trust staff. Following the opening of Mrs Greville's private rooms in 2011, it is hoped that the trust will soon open more areas of the house to the public.

What Makes Polesden Lacey Very Famous?

'Better a beeress than a peeress' was apparently Mrs Greville's attitude towards her fortune. Referred to by Cecil Beaton as a 'galumphing, greedy, snobbish old toad,' Mrs. Greville was the grand name of Edwardian society and a proud fascist. She rubbed shoulders with the richest, most famous, and most influential people of her day, wowing her guests with decadent feasts and unending hospitality. Mrs. Greville's legacy can be found in written accounts of her life, the re-telling of her favorite anecdotes, and in the conserved and restored beauty of the Polesden Lacey interiors she carefully chose.

Featured in TV and Film

- Scandalous (1984)
- Shooting Fish (1997)
- Midsomer Murders (1997) TV Series
- Close My Eyes (2001)
- Agatha Christie's Marple (2004) TV Series

Further Research

- Sian Evans, Mrs Ronnie: The Society Hostess who collected Kings (2013)

- National Trust, Polesden Lacey (2008)

Visiting Information

Polesden Lacey is open seven days a week between the months of March and October. The house is open to the public between the hours of 11 am and 5 pm, and the gardens, cafe, and shop are open from 10 am. During the winter months, the house is open by tour appointment only on weekends between the hours of 11 am and 3 pm. There is no admission charge to access the cafe, shop, and the many walking routes around the Polesden Lacey estate.

Polesden Lacey is just 25 miles from Gatwick Airport. If traveling from the airport by car, use the M23 North. Take M25 to Leatherhead, then take exit 9. On the Leatherhead By-Pass Rd, take A246 to Dorking Rd in Great Bookham. From there, directions are complex, so use a map, sat nav, or online route finder for assistance. If traveling by train, you can use the Boxhill & Westhumble, Bookham, Dorking, or Leatherhead stations. There are taxi ranks at Dorking and Leatherhead stations. London buses 478, 479, and 489 are available from Guildford of Leatherhead to Great Bookham.

For more detailed information, visit the websitehttp://www.nationaltrust.org.uk/polesden-lacey

LUTON HOO
The Great House Turned Hotel

Key Facts about Luton Hoo

- Luton Hoo is located within the parish of Hyde, Bedfordshire, close to the towns of Luton, Harpenden, and Hertfordshire.
- There has been a house on the site of Luton Hoo since at least 1601.
- The current mansion house was built for the 3rd Earl of Bute in 1767. Building work commenced in 1767.

Luton Hoo mansion house has been re-built and re-modelled by some of the finest architects to work in England. The house has seen visits from royalty such as Queen Mary, Edward VII, and Queen Elizabeth II and has been owned by a Prime Minister and Russian aristocrat. Today, you can go to Luton Hoo and spend the night, play a few holes of golf, or have a manicure as the 17th-century mansion house is now a five-star hotel, golf club, and spa.

The early history of Luton Hoo is unclear. A family named de Hoo are thought to have lived in a manor house on the site of Luton Hoo from around the year 1050 to 1450 but there is no mention of it in the Domesday Book. The Luton Hoo estate passed through the hands of many families in the succeeding years until finally being sold to John Stuart, 3rd Earl of Bute, in 1762. Bute was Prime Minister to King George III for just one year before giving up his unhappy position to focus on his large, new Bedfordshire Estate.

Robert Adams, neoclassical architect and designer to the very crème de la crème of 18th-century society, was employed by the 3rd Earl of Bute to build a magnificent new house on the site of the existing one. However, the original grandiose plans were never fully executed as parts of the original house were saved, and the new house became a large remodeling of the older one. Capability Brown was brought on board to remodel the extensive gardens and parkland, which at that time was around 300 acres but today extends to 1,065 acres of land. Ambitiously, Brown challenged Mother Nature, changing the lay of the land by damming the River Lea and forming two lakes. Despite the best efforts of a devastating fire that broke out in Luton Hoo in 1771, the Earl was resident in his new mansion by 1774 and lived there happily with his family until his death.

In 1830, when in the possession of the 3rd Earl's grandson, the 2nd Marquess of Bute, Luton Hoo was drastically transformed by the architect Sir Robert Smirke, the same architect who brought the British Museum to life. In deference to Robert Adams's original design, Smirke added a massive portico to the property, similar to Robert Adams's original but never executed plans. Smirke's remodeling of the exterior and layout of Luton Hoo uses a neo-classical style, not dissimilar to Adams, to create an imposing mansion that is nonetheless welcomingly domestic.

Another fire blitzed through Luton Hoo in 1843, destroying much of its contents. The building was a shell when John Leigh, a Liverpool solicitor, bought the estate and set about the task of rebuilding Luton Hoo yet again. The Leigh family held onto Luton Hoo until 1903, when it was purchased by diamond magnate Sir Julius Wernher. Wernher injected a new lease of life into the house, commissioning Charles Mewes and Arthus Davis, known for their creation of the Ritz Hotel in London, to redesign the interiors. The result was a lavish Edwardian Belle Époque style that provided the elaborate backdrop for the Wernher's many treasures. Mewes and Davis installed a curved marble staircase, at the center of which stands Bergonzoli's statue, 'The Love of Angels,' and their epic Great Hall, which is painted a calming blue and features Louis XV furniture and Sevres porcelain.

Sir Julius Wernher's son married Countess Anastasia Mikhailovna de Torby in 1917. 'Lady Zia,' as she was commonly known, was a member of the former Russian Imperial family and greatly added to Luton Hoo's already impressive painting and decorative art collection. Amongst her additions was an unrivaled collection of works by Russian Imperial court jeweler Peter Carl Faberge, many of which were stolen in the 1990s. An exhibition of the finest pieces in Sir Harold and Lady Zia's collection was displayed in the house in 1951.

Luton Hoo played an integral role in Second World War operations when it was used as Headquarters for the Eastern Command. In 1948, Sir Winston Churchill visited Luton Hoo and addressed over 110,000 people, thanking them for their support during the Second World War.

On Lady Zia's death in 1973, Luton Hoo passed to their elder grandson, Nicholas Phillips. Phillips died suddenly in 1991, leaving debts that forced the sale of the Luton Hoo to the Elite Hotels chain. The Luton Hoo House collection was removed and is now on display at Ranger's House in London, where the house was converted into the Luton Hoo Hotel, Golf and Spa.

What makes Luton Hoo Famous?

Luton Hoo has existed in many guises: a family home, a burnt-out shell, an opulent Edwardian palace, and now, a five-star hotel. A painstaking restoration and a £60,000,000 investment have ensured Luton Hoo is as grand and stately as any of its inhabitants could have dreamed. Luton Hoo played a key role in Second World War operations, was the home of a prime minister and a member of the Russian Imperialist Royal family, and is now a popular shooting location, appearing in many films and TV shows.

Featured in TV and Film

- Mr Turner (2014)
- War Horse (2011)
- Little Dorrit (2008) TV Series
- Bleak House (2005) TV Series

- Enigma (2001)
- Sexy Beast (2000)
- Eyes Wide Shut (1999)
- The World is Not Enough (1999)
- Four Weddings and a Funeral (1994)
- The Secret Garden (1993)

Further Research

- Raleigh Trevelyn (2012) Grand Dukes and Diamonds: The Wernhers of Luton Hoo
- Sir Harold Wernher (1955) Luton Hoo

Visiting Information

Luton Hoo is a luxury five-star hotel, golf club, and spa. Luton Hoo is just 10 minutes from Luton Airport, 70 minutes from Heathrow, and 40 minutes from Gatwick. If traveling by road, use the postcode LU1 3TQ and leave the M1 motorway at Junction 10. Drive along the dual carriageway to the Kidney Wood roundabout and take the 3rd exit to A1081. If traveling by train, Luton Parkway Station is accessible from London and is a 5-minute taxi ride away from Luton Hoo. Taxi and Car hire are available from Luton Hoo. Visit the website www.lutonhoo.co.uk for more information.

iii

PETWORTH HOUSE
A Stunning House in Sussex Made Famous by Turner

Key Facts about Petworth

- There has been a house on the site of Petworth House in Petworth, West Sussex, since the early 14th
- The current Petworth House was built in 1682 by Charles Seymour, the 6th Duke of Somerset.
- Petworth House and Estate was handed to the nation in 1947 and is now managed by the National Trust.

Petworth House is one of the most striking country houses in England. The long, imposing stone facade of the house fronts a huge number of rooms and the outbuildings, parks and mighty stone wall erected around the Petworth estate challenges the nearby town with its scale. Imagine living in this aristocratic palace with ordinary townsfolk going about their business on the other side of a vast stone wall, complete with a classical gate. The first and most famous of Petworth's inhabitants, Charles Seymour, nicknamed the 'Proud Duke,' must have imagined, liked what he saw, and then set about making it a reality.

In the early 14th century, Henry de Percy, a medieval English nobleman, chose the site of Petworth House to build his fortified manor house. A chapel dating back to this original building and the undercroft of the Great Hall are the only remains of the house that was the seat of the Percys until 1682.

The Petworth House we can see today came into being as

the result of a conceited Duke and a questionable marriage. In the year 1670, Petworth was part of the endless estates of the Duke of Northumberland, whose only heir was his daughter, Elizabeth. A dubious gift, Elizabeth's inheritance led to her being married off three times before she reached the age of sixteen. Her first husband, Henry Cavendish, died, and her second, Thomas Thynne, was murdered, the circumstances of which were never fully explained, but her marriage to her third husband, Charles Seymour, lasted until her death.

The Duke and Duchess were said to be amongst Queen Anne's closest friends, an idea vindicated by the Duchess's role as Mistress of the Robes from 1710 to 1714. The infamous couple's influence on courtly life and involvement in the many scandals of Queen Anne's reign are renowned. The 'Proud Duke,' as he was dubbed due to his attitude towards servants, townspeople, and anyone he considered beneath him, used Elizabeth's fortune to build a house worthy of the man he believed himself to be.

French-influenced, the long facade of Petworth House is devoid of architectural flourish, while the back of the house is an eclectic mix of periods, styles, and shapes. As well as the magnificent West front of the house, Charles Seymour is responsible for Petworth House's marble hall, which is the only part of the 17th-century interiors to survive a devastating fire that gutted the house in 1714.

Aside from the carnage of the fire, many of Somerset's successors altered the interiors of Petworth House dramatically throughout the next two centuries. In 1751, three years after Charles Seymour's death, famous landscape gardener Capability Brown was enlisted to design Petworth's gardens. Brown's alterations to the outside of Petworth House led to the need for alterations inside, and a new entrance had to be built on the east side. As a result, Petworth House has two entrances, two Great Halls, and two grand staircases. One of the staircases survives from Somerset's 17th-century house and features murals depicting the myth of Pandora and The Triumph of the Duchess of Somerset, both by Laguerre.

Somerset House passed to the Wyndham Family (later Egremont and Leconfield), who added to Seymour's already nationally

significant collection of paintings. The Third Earl of Egremont made perhaps the biggest contribution to Petworth House with his commission of the Carved Room, considered the jewel of Petworth. Here, ornately carved frames by Grinling Gibbon, John Selden, and Jonathan Ritson line the walls that have recently been restored back to their original 18th-century picture hang.

The rooms at Petworth are hung with the usual yet no less impressive mix of Old Master landscapes and family portraits, common in National Trust country houses. The Turner Room, however, is completely unique. In the 1830s, the Third Earl of Egremont invited friend and painter J.M.W. Turner to Petworth numerous times, offering him accommodation and a studio in which to paint. The result was over 30 extraordinary oil paintings that remain on display in the house in which they were built, as well as many others sold or loaned to galleries around the world.

Petworth House is still owned by the Egremont family, who live in the South Wing, while the remainder of the house and parks are managed by the National Trust. A Petworth Cottage Museum exists alongside Petworth House in the nearby town, offering a look into the lives of working-class estate workers around 1910.

What Makes Petworth House Famous?

Built by the infamously 'proud' 6th Duke of Somerset and his wife, the Duchess of Somerset, Mistress of the Robes and lifelong confidante to Queen Anne, Petworth House's fame stretches back to the fascinating lives of its first inhabitants. A house fit for a Duke and Duchess with serious royal connections, Petworth House, offered refuge to Queen Anne in 1692 after a typically Stuart family quarrel with William III. Petworth House's incredible collection of paintings and objects, which includes the only original terrestrial globe by Emery Molyneux and numerous oils by J.M.W. Turner, draw in visitors from all over the world.

Anglotopia's Take

We were lucky to visit around the time the film Mr Turner came out, so Petworth was having its 'moment.' They had a special exhibition with some Turner paintings and sketches. While the house is amazing and well worth exploring on its own, it contains a magnificent art collection - including several key paintings by Turner himself (including the famous panels he did of the estate, for the estate). Visit for the house, and stay for the art. You could spend an entire day here and still not see everything. Look out for special tours of the areas of the house normally closed to visitors. It's like stepping back in time.

Featured in TV and Film

- Maleficent (2014)
- Mr Turner (2014)
- Secrets of the Manor House (2012) TV Series
- Elizabeth: The Golden Age (2007)
- Barry Lyndon (1975)

Further Research

- Lydia Greeves, Great Houses of the National Trust (2015)
- Christopher Rowell, Petworth House; The People and the Place (2012)
- David Blayney Brown, Turner at Petworth (2002)
- National Trust Guidebooks, Petworth House (1997)
- Holmes, G. S., British politics in the age of Anne (1967)

Visiting Information

Petworth House is open to the public from March to September from 11 am to 5 pm. The Pleasure Gardens, Cafe, and Shop are open to the public all year round from 10 am to 5 pm.

The nearest major airport to Petworth is Gatwick, just 28 miles away. If traveling to Petworth by car, use the postcode GU28 9LR. Follow signs from the center of Petworth; the park is located on the A283. Pulbrough is the closest train station and is less than 6 miles from the property; a No. 1 Stagecoach service between Worthing and Midhurst passes Pulbrough station.

For more detailed information, visit the website, http://www.nationaltrust.org.uk/petworth-house.

CALKE ABBEY
A Perfectly Preserved Great House On the Decline

Key Facts about Calke Abbey

- There has been a building on the site of Calke Abbey since around the year 1115.
- The house and estate were owned by the Harpur Family for over 350 years.
- Calke Abbey has been owned by the National Trust since 1991 and is open to the public.

A few miles from Ticknall in Derbyshire, England, stands a grade-1 listed mansion that dates back to 1701. The house was all but forgotten for decades and slid into disrepair at the hands of the owners, who couldn't afford the upkeep of a baroque mansion in the 20th century. When the National Trust took over, Calke Abbey was best described as an old curiosity shop, filled with the cultural detritus of the same family over 300 years. Preserved in the state in which it was found and offering a glimpse of life in a country house well past its heyday, Calke Abbey is one of the most unusual National Trust properties in the UK.

Calke Abbey was never actually an Abbey, but the site was home to an Augustine Priory, founded by the 2nd Earl of Chester Richard d'Avranches around 1115. Initially an independent community dedicated to Saint Giles, little is known of the uses of Calke Priory during the later medieval period. Calke Priory, like all priories of its type, was seized by the crown during Henry VIII's Dissolution of the Monasteries and, in the succeeding years, passed

through various leasehold and freehold owners until falling into the hands of Richard Wendsley in 1575. The Elizabethan mansion he built on the site of Calke Priory forms the core of the Calke Abbey we can see today.

After a few generations of the Wendsley family, the house was bought by Sir Henry Harpur, 1st Baronet. Again, it was passed down through generations until, in 1701, it was inherited by Sir John Harpur, 4th Baronet, who rebuilt Calke Abbey on a grand scale. The new Calke Abbey was built around a central courtyard with an exterior of Derbyshire stone; it was during the ownership of the next few generations of the Harpur family that the interiors of Calke Abbey were at their finest.

From 1701 until Calke Abbey passed into the ownership of the National Trust in 1991, the house was hardly changed by its inhabitants. Sir Vauncey Harpur-Crew was the 10th and last baronet to reside at Calke Abbey. He dedicated his life to the study of natural history and the collection of taxidermy and other biological specimens. Despite the need for the 10th baronet's daughter, Hilda Harpur-Crewe, to sell much of his collection to pay his death duties, Calke Abbey continued to function partly as a home and partly as a museum of his interests.

As the exterior of the building fell into disrepair, the rooms inside were filled with belongings left behind by family members who had passed away. The effect was one of a giant time-warped family attic filled with objects, many commonplace in their time, some extraordinary in any time. The death duties demanded after the death of Charles Harpur-Crewe in 1985 finally crippled the Harpur-Crewe family's finances, and Charles's younger brother Henry Harpur-Crewe transferred the dilapidated property to the National Trust.

Unusually, the National Trust viewed Calke Abbey's state of decline as worthy of preservation and made no attempt to restore the property to its former Elizabethan glory. Instead, a massive conservation project was carried out in an attempt to freeze the property as it was, protecting it against further deterioration but retaining its state of glorious, chaotic decay.

The entrance to the house is on the ground floor and

consists of a hall hung with the trophy heads of the Harpur-Crewe's prize cattle. The main saloon is still grand and spacious and, like almost every room of the house, features various forms of taxidermy, including a crocodile's head. The caricature room features Georgian cartoons pasted directly onto the walls, and the drawing room, library, and bedrooms are all crammed full of an assortment of furnishings, household items, and curios.

Amongst the mêlée of objects to be found within Calke Abbey, one thing in particular stands out – the Calke bed. Unwanted gifts, left unopened in the bottom of wardrobes or under the bed, are common, but within Calke Abbey, these gifts have been left undisturbed for up to 300 years. A set of Chinese embroidered silk bed hangings were discovered in one of the rooms of Calke Abbey by historian Sir Howard Colvin in the early 1980s. It is thought these hangings were a gift from George II's daughter, Princess Anne, to Lady Caroline Manners. As they had never been opened, these hangings, believed to date back to 1715, were in pristine condition and remain one of the best-preserved examples of Chinese silk from this period. The Calke bed was displayed at the Treasures of Britain exhibition in Washington in 1985.

What Makes Calke Abbey Famous?

Once a dusty, forgotten mansion surrounded by a deer park in the Derbyshire Hills, Calke Abbey is now a carefully conserved and unique example of a British country house in decline. For centuries inhabited by colorful aristocratic characters, the house and estate are now a snapshot of the point at which the aristocracy became obsolete. Calke Estate is also home to a nature reserve with large woodland that has been left largely untended and undisturbed over the last three centuries.

Anglotopia's Take

This is my personal favorite stately home in Britain and National Trust property. The house being left in its state of 'arrested decay' is a brilliant and amazing way to experience a great house left in its context by the previous inhabitants. It has the most wonderful old smell. I don't know if the National Trust can keep it in this state. Visit as soon as you can. Spend the entire day, explore the house and explore the grounds. It's a magical place, and I can't wait to go back one day.

Further Research

- Calke Abbey: The National Trust Guidebook (1989)
- Howard Colvin, The Squire of Calke Abbey: The Journals of Sir George Crewe (1815-1834) (1995)

Visiting Information

Calke Abbey House is open to the public during the summer months between March and October from 12.30 pm to 5 pm every day except Thursday and Friday. During the winter months, the house is closed, but Calke Park, the restaurant, and the shop are open.

Calke Abbey is located on the A514 at Ticknall between the towns of Swadlincote and Melbourne; the postcode is DE73 7LE. If traveling by car, Calke Abbey is accessible from the M42/A42 by taking exit 13 for A50 Derby South and following the signs from there. Trains are available from Derby and Burton on Trent, and buses are available from Swadlincote. For more detailed information, visit the website: http://www.nationaltrust.org.uk/calke-abbey.

WARWICK CASTLE
A Stunning Medival Stone Castle Preserved in Warwickshire

Key Facts about Warwick Castle

- Warwick Castle is located in the town of Warwick in Warwickshire, England.
- Built in the 12th century, the Medieval stone castle was developed from an original wooden structure built by William the Conqueror in 1068.
- Owned by the Beaumont, Beauchamp, Neville, Plantagenet, Dudley, and Greville Families, Warwick Castle was sold to Merlin Entertainments, owner of Madame Tussauds, in 1978.

The site of Warwick Castle has a history that stretches way back to the year 914 when an Anglo-Saxon Burh was established by Ethelfleda, daughter of Alfred the Great. Throughout the next 1200 years, this plot of land and the buildings erected upon it have played an integral part in many major happenings of English History. Some castles in the UK are still the residences of the aristocratic families who have owned them for generation upon generation, while some are now corporate-owned tourist attractions. Unfortunately, Warwick Castle is the latter but is owned by the famous Tussaud's group, who have created well-researched and engaging displays showing life as lived at Warwick throughout the centuries.

Situated on the bend of the River Avon, Warwick Castle was built throughout the 12th and 13th centuries in the form of a shell keep, with all of its buildings located within a curtain wall. The original wooden motte-and-bailey castle erected by William the Conqueror survives to this day on a mound of land behind the castle.

Henry de Beaumont, the first owner of Warwick Castle, was made the first Earl of Warwick in 1088. What follows is four centuries of challenges to the throne, changing alliances, imprisonments, executions, and war. The Beauchamp family and later the Neville family were significant figures in baronial England and were credited with playing a key role in the Game of Thrones that typified the English Middle Ages. Warwick Castle was a key stronghold at the center of every great alliance and treachery and had to be fortified against its enemies.

Huge modifications and extensions of the stone castle were made by the Beauchamp family from 1330 to 1360. The castle's defenses were enhanced with an outer wall secluding its entire length from the nearby town, the addition of a fortified gateway (barbican), and a gatehouse, as well as three towers known as Caesar's Tower, Guy's Tower, and the Watergate Tower.

The last of the Beauchamp line was Anne de Beauchamp, 15th Countess of Warwick. Following the countess's death, Warwick Castle passed by inheritance to Richard Neville, known in his later years as the 'Kingmaker.' After deposing not one but two kings during the War of the Roses, Neville rebelled against King Edward IV, imprisoned him in Warwick Castle, and took it upon himself to rule England in the King's name. Eventually, Neville released the King and later met his end at the Battle of Baronet, ceding Warwick Castle to the crown.

Under the care of the crown, the castle was repaired, and King Richard III ordered the construction of the Bear and Clarence towers, designed as artillery bases and independent strongholds from the rest of the castle. Warwick Castle today has retained and embellished its appearance during medieval times. Visitors can see recreations of the castle's torture chamber, dungeon, armories, and stables, as well as explore original turrets, ramparts, and the notoriously haunted tower.

In 1604, King James I awarded Warwick Castle to Sir Fulke Greville, who turned the military stronghold into a country house and restored various parts of the castle in a magnificent Jacobean style. Enjoying the fruits of his labor doesn't last long as Fulke Greville is murdered in the castle by his servant, who is said to have been enraged by the discovery that he had been left out of Fulke Greville's will. His ghost is said to have haunted the castle tower ever since.

Next under the ownership of Robert Greville, 2nd Baron Brooke and known parliamentarian, Warwick Castle came under siege from Royalist forces during the English Civil War. Following yet another period of unrest and a long period of abandonment, the castle was given to Francis Greville, 8th Baron Brooke, who employed Capability Brown to landscape the castle's gardens and Italian painter Canaletto to paint the castle's interiors.

The Georgian era is the next period of history immortalized within Warwick Castle's many walls, with a whole suite of reception rooms decorated in 18th-century tapestries and furnishings. A bedroom was decorated especially for a visit from Queen Anne in 1704, although she never actually turned up. The residential and primarily Victorian part of the castle contains a dining room, chapel, and Great Hall, which features the celebrated Kenilworth Buffet, an epic carving depicting Queen Elizabeth I's legendary arrival at Kenilworth Castle to meet her admirer, Dudley.

The final moment in Warwick's history to be preserved in a tableau of authentic interiors and waxworks is the Edwardian 'royal weekend party,' which consists of a display of dinner guests based on an authentic 1898 guest list, including the Prince of Wales and the Dukes of Devonshire and Marlborough and their wives.

In 1978, Warwick Castle was purchased by entertainment company the Tussauds Group and has operated as a tourist attraction ever since. The castle is a scheduled ancient monument and grade I-listed building and, as such, is protected against unauthorized changes.

Why is Warwick Castle Famous?

Warwick Castle and its long line of powerful and influential owners have had a part to play in all of the major English conflicts between the 13th and 20th centuries. Created as a result of the

Norman Conquest, Warwick Castle has seen action in the Hundred Years' War, the Wars of the Roses, and the English Civil War and remained standing. With over 36 individual owners over the years, the castle has seen major renovations and alterations over the last 950 years and now exists as a popular historical tourist attraction.

Featured in TV and Film

- Nativity 2: Danger in the Manger (2012)
- The Virgin Queen (2005) TV Mini-series
- Magnificent Monuments (2000) TV Series
- Macbeth (1997)
- King Ralph (1991)
- Antiques Roadshow (1979) TV Series
- The Back Rose (1950)
- Prince Valiant (1954)

Further Research

- Marc Morris (2012) Castle: A History of the Buildings that Shaped Medieval Britain
- Dan Jones (2013) The Plantagenets
- Warwick Frances Evelyn Mayna (2013) Warwick Castle and Its Earls, from Saxon Times to the Present Day
- Llewelyn Jewitt (2013) Warwick Castle: A Nineteenth Century Perspective
- Sushila Anand (2009) Daisy: The Life and Loves of the Countess of Warwick

Visiting Information

Warwick Castle is open to the public all year round, but opening times vary depending on the day and events scheduled. A standard adult ticket costs £18, and a child ticket costs £15.60. Warwick Castle is located just 40 40-minute drive from Birmingham International Airport. If traveling by car, use the M40 motorway and exiting at junction 15; the castle is just two miles away. For sat nav, use the postcode CV34 6AH. If traveling by rail from London, use Warwick Station, which is one mile from the castle. A direct train line is also available from Birmingham Snow Hill.

For more information, view the website www.warwick-castle.com

CLIVEDEN HOUSE
The House Made Notorious by Political Scandal

Key Facts about the House

- Cliveden Mansion and Estate is located at Taplow, Buckinghamshire, England.
- The present house was built in 1851 by architect Charles Barry
- There have been three houses built on this site, the first in 1666.
- The present house was once home to Nancy Astor and the meeting place for the Cliveden Set in the 1920s and 1930s.

Once home to one of the most famous cliques in British history, the 'Cliveden Set,' Cliveden House is a country mansion that boasts some of the most impressive gardens in the country and a history peppered with political scandal. Built-in a mixture of English Palladium and Italian Roman Cinquento style that overlooks the River Thames, Cliveden House is currently a very impressive, very exclusive hotel.

Cliveden House is an Italianate mansion overlooking the mighty River Thames in Buckinghamshire in the South of England. In 1666, the first house was built on this site by architect William Wilde to specifications set by the 2nd Duke of Buckingham, the main instruction being to capture the spectacular riverside view. This early house was destroyed by a fire in 1795, and, remarkably, so was the second house built on this site, which lasted from 1824 until its demise in 1849.

Following the fire of 1849, the 2nd Duke of Sutherland

decided to rebuild the house with the help of architect Sir Charles Barry, best known for his work on the British Houses of Parliament. The architectural design for Cliveden retained some elements of the first and second houses, including a medieval hall and viewing platform that dates back to the seventeenth century. The mansion is built over three stories in a blend of English Palladian style and Roman Cinquecento with an exterior that resembles an Italianate villa. The roof of the mansion was designed to be walked upon, affording spectacular views across Buckinghamshire and Berkshire. The later addition of a grand 100-foot clock tower was designed by Henry Clutton and is actually a water tower that is still in use today.

The gardens at Cliveden are some of the largest and most beautiful in the country. The formal Parterre is still one of the largest in Europe and dates back to 1723 when Cliveden was owned by the Earl of Orkney. The current gardens are based on the designs of head gardener John Fleming, who worked with the house's architect, Charles Barry, to create a complex system of seasonal flower beds in the late 19th century. As well as the grand Parterre, current visitors can enjoy Cliveden's Rose Garden, Japanese Water Garden, Long Garden, Sculpture, Maze, and Woodlands.

Located up river from Windsor Castle, Cliveden is said to have been frequented by Queen Victoria during the 1850s but in 1868, following the Duke's death in 1861, Lady Sutherland passed away and the house was sold to the Duke of Westminister. In 1893, the Duke sold Cliveden to the wealthy American William Waldorf Astor. Following some incredible alterations, such as the installation of a Rococo French dining room from the Chateau d'Asnieres outside Paris and the addition of a complete balustrade from the Villa Borghese in Rome, Astor gave Cliveden to his son Waldorf 1906, on the event of his marriage to fellow American Nancy Shaw, and moved to Hever Castle.

During the years the young Astors owned and resided in Cliveden, the house became notorious for the influential guests and lavish entertainment of the young couple's regular house parties. The heyday of the Cliveden social scene was between the two world wars when the Astors were said to entertain some of the most famous and powerful entertainers, writers, and politicians of the time. The 'Cliveden set' as the Astor's more prominent, aristocratic guests became known, were said to be politically influential and controversial advocates of the appeasement of Hitler's Germany in the years leading up to World War Two.

During the First World War, the grounds of Cliveden became home to the HRH Duchess of Connaught Hospital, a Canadian Red Cross hospital for the treatment of wounded soldiers. The hospital was dismantled in 1918 but rebuilt under the name of the Canadian Red Cross Memorial Hospital at the outbreak of World War Two. The hospital remained following the end of the war and was in use up until the 1980s, focussing on maternity, nursing, and rheumatology. The grounds of Cliveden are also home to Cliveden War Cemetery, where 42 Commonwealth citizens are buried.

Cliveden was gifted by the Astors to the National Trust in 1942, along with an endowment of £250,000, but the Astors continued to live there until 1968. Following Bill Astor's death, Cliveden was let to Stanford University until, in 1985, it was restored, refurbished, and re-opened as a luxury hotel. In the years from 1985 to today, Cliveden has passed through many hands and was most recently purchased in 2012 by London and Regional Properties.

What Makes This House Very Famous

Currently, the Cliveden Hotel's motto is "Nothing ordinary ever happened here, nor could it." Cliveden entered the collective consciousness of Britain, if not Europe, in the 1930s due to it being the setting of the famous social gatherings of the 'Cliveden Set.' This group of aristocratic personalities, which included politician William Montagu, Lord Halifax, Lord Lothian, and Geoffrey Dawson, editor of The Times newspaper, are said to have had an influential role in political decision-making in the lead-up to the Second World War and have been accused of being allied to Nazism. The Profumo Scandal of 1963 lent even greater infamy to Cliveden after a cottage on the house's estate was said to be the setting of Secretary of State for War John Profumo's 'immoral' relationship with 19-year-old model Christine Keeler.

Cliveden in Film

Cliveden has been used as a location in the following films.

- Sherlock Holmes (2009) Film
- Made of Honour (2008) Film
- Mrs Henderson Presents (2005) Film
- Thunderbirds (2004) Film
- Dead Man's Folly (1986) Film
- Death of the Nile (1978) Film
- Help! (1965) Film
- The Card (1952) Film

Further Research

- James Craythorne (1995) Cliveden: The Place and the People
- National Trust (2002) Cliveden
- Norman Rose (2001) The Cliveden Set: Portrait of an Exclusive Fraternity
- Clive Aslet (2013) An Exuberant Catalogue of Dreams: The Americans Who Revived the Country House in Britain

Visitor Information

Cliveden's gardens and woodlands, complete with various cafes and shops, are looked after by the National Trust and are open to the public from 10 am to 5 pm every day. Cliveden House is now a luxury hotel, but tours of parts of the ground floor are available on Thursdays and Sundays between 3 pm and 5.30 pm from April to October. For more information visithttp://www.nationaltrust.org.uk/cliveden

BOLSOVER CASTLE
A Stunning Castle in Derbyshire

Key Facts about Bolsover Castle

- Bolsover Castle is located in Bolsover, Derbyshire, England.
- A castle was built on this site in the 12th century by the Peveral Family and became property of the crown in 1155.
- Bolsover Castle was rebuilt by Sir Charles Cavendish in 1608.
- Now in the care of English Heritage and designated a Grade I listed building, Bolsover Castle is a Scheduled Ancient Monument.

Part 12th-century medieval palace ruins and part 17th-century Elizabethan renaissance mansion, Bolster Castle in Derbyshire is a unique and internationally important structure. Once home to Cavalier playboy Sir William Cavendish, who entertained King Charles I within its walls, Bolsover Castle has an intriguing past and earned its place in history with its role during the English Civil War.

Bolsover Castle was built by the Peverel family in the 12th century but soon fell into the hands of the crown. Various revolts and conflicts of the 12th century played out at Bolsover Castle. Ownership passed between the crown and the succeeding Ferrer family for many years until, in 1290, Bolsover Castle was given to local farmers who allowed it to fall into a state of disrepair.

Using this earlier, decrepit castle keep as a basic design, Sir Charles Cavendish, son of Bess of Hardwick, bought Bolsover Castle and Manor in 1608 and set about re-building it. Working with John Smithson, Charles Cavendish set about a major renovation of the existing castle in 1612 and added the tower, known as The Little Castle, which was completed in 1621. Charles didn't live to see his project to fruition, and when he died in 1616, his son, William Cavendish, who later became Duke of Newcastle Upon Tyne, resumed the building.

Bolsover's Little Castle was designed to be the embodiment of Elizabethan Renaissance beauty and refinement. It was a structure intended for the purposes of entertainment and fine living and has the look of a fairytale palace rather than a medieval fortress. With William Cavendish in charge, John Smythson added a riding house with an inner courtyard and a small palace to the original design, both impressive examples of authentic Stuart architecture.

The contrasting architectural styles employed in the original 12th-century building of Bolsover Castle and its Cavendish redevelopment in the 17th century are best admired with a walk through the Great Court. The Little Castle features a Renaissance 'Romeo and Juliet' style window that overlooks a lawn. The interiors of the Little Castle are said to be a startling example of Elizabethan Romanticism, and its stone chambers are part medieval and part Renaissance in style.

The interiors of Bolsover Castle are a shrine to the late-Elizabethan obsession with medieval chivalry, knights and ladies, and courtly love. The hall in the Little Castle is complete with a mock Gothic fireplace, vaulted ceiling, and mural of the Labours of Hercules. Just off the entrance, there is an ante-room that features wall paintings of the four medieval humors: melancholic, choleric, phlegmatic, and sanguine. Murals of the senses follow in the adjacent Pillar Parlour, which is said to have been based on the Great Parlour of the Cecil Palace of the Theobalds in Hertfordshire. The upstairs Star Chamber features a geometrically paneled ceiling painted blue and peppered with stars, wall paintings of Old Testament figures, and whole rooms dedicated to the depiction of Heaven and Elysium. The ceiling paintings in these rooms are said to have been painted in shell gold, which was '400 times more expensive than gold leaf'.

William Cavendish himself was known to be quite a character, a Cavalier playboy concerned solely with courtly life, riding, and traveling Europe. During the civil war, he was called upon to defend the North for the King but failed at Marsden Moor in 1644 and fled for the continent. Bolsover Castle was taken by the Parliamentarians, who allowed it to fall into a ruinous state, but following the Restoration, Cavendish returned and, by the time he died in 1676, had restored the castle to its former glory.

Bolsover Castle became derelict around 1883 after descendants of Cavendish moved the contents to their seat at Welbeck. The Little Castle was used as a rectory for a spell during the 19th century before being given to the government by the 7th Duke of Portland in 1945. Now looked after by English Heritage, Bolsover Castle is recognized as a nationally important historical site and internationally important structure.

What Makes Bolsover Castle Famous?

An incredible example of 17th-century architecture with ruins dating back to the 12th century, Bolsover is a scheduled ancient monument and grade I listed historical building. With the look of a fairytale palace on a hill, Bolsover embodies Elizabethan Romanticism of the mid-17th century as well as being an important site during the English Civil War. In 1634, William Cavendish entertained King Charles I and his Queen at a grand masque at Bolsover Castle, which is said to have bankrupted him for the rest of his life. This event and others held within the walls of this eccentric castle tell the story of the tensions between king and state in the early 17th century that eventually led to civil war in England.

Bolsover Castle on Film and TV

Bolsover Castle has appeared in the following films and TV shows.

- Secret Knowledge: Bolsover Castle with Lucy Worsley (2014) TV Show
- Jane Eyre (2006) TV adaptation

Further Reading

- Worsley, Lucy (2001) Bolsover Castle
- Paul Drury (2014) Bolsover Castle (English Heritage Red Guides)
- John Hamilton and T Thorneley (2010) Bolsover Castle 1883
- Stuart Reid and Graham Turner (2006) Castles and Tower Houses of the Scottish Clans 1450-1650

Visiting Information

Bolsover Castle is run by English Heritage and is open to the public between 10.00 am and 6.00 pm every day during the summer period from the 1st of April to the 30th of September. From October, opening times change each month. Entry for English Heritage members is free. For more information, visit the website www.english-heritage.org.uk/daysout/properties/bolsover-castle/.

HOLKHAM HALL
A Stunning Palladian House

Key Facts About Holkham Hall

- Holkham Hall is located opposite the village of Holkham in Norfolk, England.
- The first foundations for the country house were laid in 1734, but the building was not completed until 1764.
- Holkham Hall was built by the 1st Earl of Leicester, Thomas Coke, and remains the family home of the Earls of Leicester of Holkham.

With one of the finest private collections of sculpture and paintings in the world, Holkham Hall is an art museum in its own right. An 18th-century country house built in an exquisite Palladian style, Holkham Hall is located in the heart of the Norfolk countryside and remains the private property of the current Earl of Leicester of Holkham.

Sir Edward Coke, Chief Justice to James 1st and founder of the family's fortune, purchased the Holkham Estate in 1609. One hundred thirteen years later, his descendant Thomas Coke embarked on his six-year Grand Tour of Europe and returned in 1718 with an impressive array of antiquities and some grand plans to build an English country home like no other. Sir Edward Coke is said to be responsible for the maxim 'an Englishman's home is his castle,' a sentiment his great-grandson Thomas Coke certainly took to heart when he set about designing and building one of the most impressive Palladian Revival style houses in England, bankrupting himself in the process.

During his Grand Tour, Thomas Coke (made 1st Earl of Leicester in 1744) did not only collect great works of art and literature; he collected acquaintances who included the architect William Kent and Lord Burlington, an aristocrat and architect who was known for his enthusiasm for Palladian Revival style. Briefly popular in England before the Civil War, Palladianism enjoyed a revival during the 1720s and 30s as a reaction against the popular Baroque style associated with Queen Anne. Loosely based on the work of the Italian architect Andrea Palladio, Palladianism of the early 18th century eventually evolved into the Georgian style that is still popular in English country houses today. With the encouragement and expertise of his new friends, Coke set about designing Holkham Hall in 1726, creating the 'most Italian house in England.'

Influenced by the construction of nearby Houghton Hall and aided by his assistant, local Norfolk architect Matthew Brettingham, Coke designed a yellow-brick Roman palace whose exterior was unusually severe and devoid of ornamentation, even by Palladian standards. Favoring function and efficiency over style, Holkham Hall has few windows and only two stories, the piano nobile containing a series of state rooms flanked by two purely functional courtyards. The central block is linked to four corner pavilions designed to house Coke's family, Coke's visitors, the kitchens, and a chapel.

Designed primarily by William Kent, the grandeur of Holkham Hall's interiors took 34 years to complete and have been described as the 'finest Palladian interior in England.' Thomas Coke never saw his great country house completed, as he died in 1759 before the building of the house was even complete. The finishing and furnishing of the interiors of the house were overseen by Coke's wife, Lady Margaret Tufton, Countess of Leicester.

Kent's penchant for simplicity and insistence on the eloquence of a plain surface is evident in most of Holkham Hall's grand spaces. Entrance to the house is through the epic Marble Hall, a room set over two levels with an imposing white marble staircase connecting the hall to a saloon that has been referred to as 'one of the great chambers of England.' The space was designed by Kent to imitate Palladio's design for a Temple of Justice and is made mostly from Derbyshire Alabaster. Classical niches and reliefs line the walls and give way to an incredible coffered and gilded ceiling that was inspired by the Pantheon in Rome.

The Marble Hall leads to the piano nobile and staterooms. Each of the staterooms, although furnished with a light touch, houses magnificent treasures. In the North Dining room, the Axminster carpet perfectly reflects the ceiling above, panels depicting Aesop's fables crown two marble fireplaces, and the sideboard alcove represents the apse of a Roman Basilica. The walls of the drawing room and south saloon are covered in crimson velvet and hung with paintings by Poussin, Claude, Rubens, and Van Dyck. The south dining room houses two great portraits of Thomas Coke, 1st Earl of Leicester, one by Batoni and one by Gainsborough.

The West Gallery or 'Statue Gallery' was built specifically to display Coke's collection of statuary, mostly Roman copies of Greek works purchased during Thomas Coke's Grand Tour, and The Landscape Room has been hung in the floor-to-ceiling 18th-century style, mostly with landscapes by Poussin and Claude. Finally, the state bedroom suite with walls of green damask is decorated with Brussels and Mortlake tapestries and rich embroidery hangings.

Holkham Hall's grounds are now made up of almost 3,000 acres that stretch down from the house to wild coastal marshland. William Kent began work on the grounds several years before the house was constructed, an event that was commemorated in 1730 with the construction of a 24m Obelisk. Holkham Hall is said to have cost around £90,000 when it was built, a cost that left the Coke family in debt following the 1st Earl of Leicester's death in 1759. This debt and the severe design of the house have meant that it stands now almost exactly as it did in 1764 when it was completed. Still the family home of the Earls of Leicester of Holkham, the house is open to the public for pre-arranged tours.

What Makes Holkham House Very Famous

For many, Holkham House is the finest example of Palladian architecture in England. The Holkham collection of ancient Roman marble sculptures is one of the finest private collections in the world, and its collection of paintings includes key works by Reubens, Van Dyck, Poussin, Claude, and Thomas Gainsborough. The current Earl of Leicester is a key figure in the great house's survival. There are over 300 houses on his estate, still existing in a state of tight and self-sustained community.

Holkham Hall on Film and TV

Holkham Hall has appeared in the following films and TV shows.

- Glorious 39 (2009) Film
- The Duchess (2008) Film
- Antiques Roadshow (February 2007) TV Series
- The Curious House Guest (March 2006) TV Series
- The Lost Prince (2003) TV Film
- Shakespeare in Love (1998) Film

Further Research

- Nicholas McCann (1996) Holkham Hall: Great Houses of Britain
- Schmidt and Keller (2005) Holkham
- P. Mortlock (2007) Aristocratic Splendour: Money and the world of Thomas Coke, Earl of Leicester.
- Susan Weber (2013) William Kent: Designing Georgian Britain

Visiting Information

From the 1st of April to the 31st of October, the Hall is open from 12.00 pm to 4.00 pm on Sundays, Mondays, and Thursdays. Access to the gardens and museum is available every day. See the website www.holkham.co.uk for more information.

AUDLEY END
A Stunning Example of Jacobean Architecture in Essex

Key Facts about Audley End

- Audley End House is located just outside of the town of Saffron Walden in Essex, England.
- This large country house was built on the site of the former Walden Abbey in the 17th century by Thomas Howard, the first Earl of Suffolk.
- Audley End is now under the stewardship of English Heritage.

Built to impress a king, Audley End House is a stately home with palatial aspirations and one of Britain's finest examples of 17th-century Jacobean architecture. Thanks to ambitious restoration work carried out in the Victorian era, and ongoing careful conservation, Audley End remains to this day one of the grandest and most extravagant country houses in the UK.

Audley End was once the site of a Benedictine monastery known as Walden Abbey. In 1538, during the Dissolution of the Monasteries, Henry VIII granted Walden Abbey to Lord Chancellor Sir Thomas Audley, who converted the building into a country house and renamed it Audley Inn. In 1582, Sir Thomas Audley's grandson Thomas Howard, Earl of Suffolk and one of Drake's captains, inherited the Audley estate. A rising courtier with his sights set firmly on impressing James I, the monarch at the time, Thomas Howard demolished Audley Inn and set about building a palatial Jacobean prodigy house fit for a king.

Building work began promptly in 1582 but was not complete until 1614. At a reputed cost of £200,000, a colossal sum at the time, the building of Audley House left the Howard family burdened with serious debt. The finished Audley End House was Elizabethan in style with a glamorous facade showcasing turrets, pinnacles, parapets and large windows that seem to cover the exterior. The design is symmetrical; the Great Hall bay window is centrally placed, and two porches, presumably intended for the use of the king and queen, lead to suites at either side of the house.

In 1619, Thomas Howard and his wife were found guilty of embezzlement and sent to the Tower of London for a period of one year. Howard died in disgrace at Audley End in 1626, never to receive his visit from King James I and his queen.

However, Howard's aspirations of entertaining royals were not entirely in vain, as in 1666, Audley End was leased by Charles II so he could be close to the racing at Newmarket. The money paid by the king for the use of Audley End did nothing to diminish the amount of debt hanging over the house when ownership returned to the Howards in 1701. Despite this, huge changes were made to the house, which at this time was of both the scale and grandeur of a royal palace.

Sir John Vanbrugh was employed to demolish most of the forecourt and construct a Baroque screen to the main staircase in 1708. In 1753, the East Wing was demolished, and in 1762, the new owner, Sir John Griffin, commissioned Capability Brown to landscape the grounds. Griffin also employed Robert Adams to design new reception rooms on the ground floor of Audley End and refurbish its South Wing in the grand, formal style of 18th-century classicism.

The Adams Suite was destroyed by the 3rd Lord Braybrooke in the 1830s and subsequently reinstated in the 1960s at public expense. What we see today in this English Heritage property is a thorough restoration of what Adam originally created: two drawing rooms, a lobby, and a dining room, all furnished and decorated with exquisite neo-classical finery. The Little Drawing Room is a favorite amongst visitors and is said to be amongst Adam's most impressive small works. Traditionally, ladies would have withdrawn to this room, resting under the jewel-like ornamentation covering the walls and ceiling and leaving the gentleman to continue drinking and gesticulating in the nearby Dining Parlour.

Due to the huge restoration project carried out by the 3rd Baron Braybrooke, which aimed to restore the house's original Jacobean interiors, Audley End is an eclectic Jacobean mansion with Victorian features and hints of the Elizabethan. The Great Hall is alive with a grand array of pikes, firearms, banners, and portraits and features an ornately carved Jacobean oak screen. The Grand Chamber, sometimes referred to as the Fish Room, features fantastic Jacobean plasterwork sculpted with dolphins and sea monsters, a Gothic frieze, and an Elizabethan fireplace. This room is furnished mostly in Regency, the popular saloon style of the 1820s.

Behind the Great Hall stands the picture gallery, built specifically by the 3rd Baron Braybrooke in the 1820s to display the house's huge collection of paintings. The next Lord Braybrooke to own Audley End installed his collection of stuffed animals and birds in the space, creating one of the largest taxidermy collections of any English house. The Drawing Room features paintings by van Goyen and Canaletto, and a large and rare portrait of George II hangs in the Dining Room. The Chapel is a rare example of ornamented white and ochre Gothic style, and the Howard Bedroom contains a magnificent state bed crowned with a coronet, a stool, armchairs, and a portrait of Queen Charlotte, all of which were commissioned in the late 18th century in anticipation of a royal visit.

Audley End was used by the Special Operations Executive during the Second World War and returned to the possession of the ninth Lord Braybrooke in 1945. Lord Braybrooke gifted Audley End to English Heritage in 1948 and moved into a house on the grounds where his descendants still live.

What Makes Audley End Famous?

Audley End is one of the most extravagant and expensive houses to be constructed in England in the 16th century. Built to win the favor of King James I, Audley End was owned for a time by King Charles II and so achieved its royal connection, albeit long after the original owner's death. In the mid-18th century, Robert

Adams created some of his most spectacular signature interiors at Audley House. The restoration of these rooms has been completed to such a high standard that many visit Audley End just to see the Adams rooms.

Featured in TV and Film

The following films and TV shows were filmed at Audley End

- Great British Bakeoff (2010) TV Series
- Woman of Straw (1964) Film

Further Research

- Russel Chamberlain (1986) Audley End
- Paul Drury (2010) Audley End: English Heritage Guidebooks
- Gillian Mawrey and Linden Groves (2010) The Gardens of English Heritage
- Ian Valentine (1998) Station 43: Audley End House and SOE's Polish Section

Visiting Information

Audley End House and Gardens are open to the public every day between the 1st of April and the 1st of November. Between 1st April and 30th September, Audley House is open from 12.00 pm to 17.00 pm, and the gardens are open from 10.00 am to 18.00 pm each day. Opening times change during other months. Visit the websitehttp://www.english-heritage.org.uk/daysout/properties/audley-end-house-and-gardens/ for more information.

BEAULIEU PALACE HOUSE
Home to Britain's National Motor Museum

Key Facts about Beaulieu House

- Beaulieu Palace House is located in Beaulieu, Hampshire, England.
- Originally built as the Great Gatehouse of Beaulieu Abbey, this house was built in the 13th
- The house has belonged to a branch of the Montagu Family since 1592.
- Beaulieu is still home to the current Lord and Lady Montagu but can be visited by the public.

Beaulieu Palace House, as it is grandly known, is part medieval Cistercian Abbey and part Victorian Gothic revivalist country mansion. Opened up to the public in the 1950s by the famous 3rd Baron Edward Douglas-Scott Montagu, Beaulieu House created the blueprint for other stately homes to transition from family homes to tourist destinations and exists today as part of the group of museums and attractions known as 'Beaulieu.' It's pronounced "Bewly" if you're curious and stumbling trying to remember High School French.

Beaulieu Abbey was a Cistercian Abbey founded in 1203 by King John. The buildings comprising the Abbey were so magnificent in scale and style that it took almost forty years to complete. When Henry VIII brought about the Dissolution of the Monasteries in 1538, Thomas Wriothesley, the 1st Earl of Southampton, succeeded over much competition to win the right to buy the Abbey, estates, and 3,441ha of surrounding Beaulieu lands.

Lord Southampton began building a house on the site of the Abbey, the current Beaulieu Palace House, and used the existing Grand Gatehouse building as the foundation of his mansion. The existing porch, hall, and two first-floor chapels were converted into a typical 16th-century manor house. Although Lord Southampton demolished the church, he preserved the monk's refectory, which he donated to the people of Beaulieu to be used as their parish church. The cloisters and the dormitory were also preserved and remain to this day as part of the Beaulieu Museum.

In the 19th century, Beaulieu Palace House passed into the care of the Dukes of Buccleuch and was extensively rebuilt in the 1870s. Under the expertise of Sir Arthur Blomfield, Beaulieu was transformed into a typically Victorian Gothic Revivalist country mansion. Traces of the original medieval architecture remain in the original 14th-century inner hall, now used as a dining room, which features a stone ribbed vault and linen paneling taken from the old House of Commons. But despite these medieval features the Victorian remodelling overwhelms. The two former abbey chapels were transformed into an ante-room and an upper drawing room. The drawing room is decorated with a wooden beamed roof and Gothic stenciling, and the kitchen stands exactly as it did in Victorian times.

The carefully conserved historical elements of this house do nothing to detract from the fact that Beaulieu is, first and foremost, a family home. Portraits of Montagus, old and young, historic and modern, line the walls of this house, and the guidebook contains endless details of how each of these rooms was used by Montagus past and present.

The most memorable member of the Montagu line to reside in this house is undoubtedly the 3rd Baron of Montagu, Edward Douglas-Scott Montagu, who inherited Beaulieu Palace House in 1951. At just twenty-five years old, the Baron saw how country houses across England were struggling to survive and immediately threw open his doors to the public. The Baron made an exhibit of his own family, tempting visitors into the house by revealing the house and home of an English aristocratic family. A born showman, the Baron had five antique cars placed in the entrance to the house and staged the first country house jazz festival outside.

The renovations of the 19th century also transformed the Beaulieu Gardens. Originally the grounds of the Abbey, the gardens include a Victorian flower garden, an informal wilderness garden, and an ornamental kitchen garden that features a restored 1870 vinehouse. The Beaulieu Gardens are also home to the historic Rufus Memorial Cairn. Made of stone from the Abbey ruins, the cairn is said to mark the spot where King William Rufus was shot and killed by an arrow in 1100.

Today, Beaulieu Palace House is a member of the Treasure Houses of England consortium. The houses and gardens are just two of the attractions in the surrounding area known as 'Beaulieu.' Beaulieu Palace House and Gardens, the National Motor Museum, the James Bond Experience (featuring vehicles from the films), the Secret Army Exhibition, the World of Top Gear, and a Monorail can all be visited with the purchase of one ticket.

What Makes Beaulieu Palace House Famous?

One of the many Abbeys to be bought and converted into a lavish country house by an aristocrat following Henry VIII's Dissolution of the Churches in 1538, Beaulieu Palace House is famous in part because of the family who lived within its walls. When the 3rd Baron of Montagu opened the doors of Beaulieu Palace House to the public in 1952, he did it with the full knowledge that the life of the British aristocracy, indeed the life of his own family, going back through previous generations for hundreds of years, was something the great British public was desperate to know more about. A man who enjoyed the high life, the 3rd Baron, his collection of antique cars, and his love of fine wine and jazz embodied everything people expected from an upper-class English gentleman. Ultimately, his readiness to open up his home, his life, and the lives of his family to public scrutiny made Beaulieu Palace House one of the most popular stately homes in the country. The house is also believed to be haunted by the ghosts of Lady Isabella Montagu and incense-burning monks.

Beaulieu on Film and TV

The following films and TV shows were filmed at Beaulieu House

- Churchill's Spy School (2010) Documentary
- Cassandra's Dream (2007) Film
- Mrs Palfrey at the Claremont (2005) Film
- Ghostwatch Live (2001) TV Show

Further Research

- Edward Douglas Scott Montagu (1983) Beaulieu Palace, House and Abbey
- Frederick Hockney (1976) Beaulieu, King John's Abbey: A History of Beaulieu Abbey, Hampshire 1204-1538

Visiting Information

Beaulieu is open daily from May to September between the house at 10 am and 6 pm. From October to April, the opening hours are 10 am to 5 pm. A visit to 'Beaulieu,' which includes entry to Beaulieu Palace House and Gardens, costs £21 for an adult, £12.50 for a youth, £10.50 for a child, and under five go free. By buying a ticket online in advance, you will receive a ten percent discount. Visit the website www.beaulieu.co.uk for more information.

CHEQUERS
The Country Home of Britain's Prime Minister

Key Facts about the House

- Chequers is located near Ellesborough in Buckinghamshire, England.
- Chequers was built in the 16th century by William Hawtrey.
- There has been a house on the site of Chequers since the 12th century.
- Chequers has been the private country retreat of the Prime Minister of the United Kingdom since 1921.

Chequers Court is the official country retreat of the Prime Minister of the United Kingdom. Currently enjoyed by David Cameron, Chequers is a 16th-century gothic mansion elegantly restored to its former glory by Reginald Bloomfield in the early 20th century. Once the jail of a banished royal, Chequer's rich history dates back to Elizabethan times, but its treasures are unfortunately not open to the public.

Chequers Court is known for its important role in British political life. Located just 41 miles from Downing Street, this 16th-century country house and estate was given to the nation of Great Britain in 1917 by Sir Arthur Lee and has been the official country seat and private retreat of the Prime Minister since 1921.

Chequer's origins are somewhat ambiguous. It is known that the house as it stands today was built, or at least extensively remodeled, by William Hawtrey in 1565. Hawtrey's name appears in the reception room of the house, and his initials and the date of

1565 are carved into the brickwork in various places on the house's exterior. What sort of building stood on the site of Chequers before Hawtrey's remodeling is largely unknown, but the dating of building materials suggests that there has been a house on this site since the 12th century. The name 'Chequers' may come from the house's first resident, Elias Ostiarius, whose name indicates that he was an usher of the Court of the Exchequer. This original house passed through many generations of this family before being passed into the Hawtrey family line.

In the same year, Hawtrey completed his renovations, Chequers earned its place in the great tomes of English History when it became the prison of a banished royal, the great-granddaughter of Henry VIII, Lady Mary Grey. Queen Elizabeth I herself ordered Lady Mary Grey's confinement herself when it was learned Lady Grey had married without her family's consent. For two years, between 1565 and 1567, Hawtrey guarded Lady Grey in an attempt to ensure she would have no descendants who could, in the future, challenge the throne. The room in which Lady Grey was confined has been kept in its original condition.

Chequers passed through many families in subsequent years including the Wooleys, Crokes and Thurbanes and the Russells. John Russell, owner of Chequers in 1715, was Oliver Cromwell's grandson. In 1832, the house was still in the possession of the Russell family, and it was Sir George Russell who commissioned architect William Atkinson to modernize the house in gothic style by removing Hawtrey's original Tudor paneling and windows, plastering the exterior, and redecorating the interior in a neo-gothic style.

Chequers was briefly owned by the Astley family and leased by the wonderfully named Clutterbucks before being taken on a long lease by a Mr Arthur Lee and his wife, an American heiress, Ruth Lee. With the advice of Reginald Bloomfield and the work of Bertram Astley, the Lees brought Chequers back to its original Elizabethan style. The external Gothic additions made by the Russells were removed, the Tudor features reinstated, and the interiors were remodeled using many imported and reproduction 16th and 17th-century antiquities.

In the East wing of the house sits the magnificent Hawtrey

Room, which Bloomfield restored with imported 16th-century paneling and reproduction heraldic glass. Above this room is the Great Parlour, which features a chimney brought by Lord Lee from one of his houses in Ipswich and an Elizabethan-style frieze and plasterwork. The Great Hall was also completely remodeled by Bloomfield, who added a plaster ceiling copied from the residence of Paul Pindar, an alabaster fireplace, and a 17th-century screen that forms a passage on the south side.

A few years before the outbreak of World War I, the Lees purchased Chequers and allowed the house to be used as a hospital during wartime. Following the war, the Lees, who were by this time the Lord and Lady of Fareham and childless, left the house to the nation. On 8 January 1921, the Lees handed over the house to then-Prime Minister David Lloyd George. A stained glass window in Chequers has the following inscription: "This house of peace and ancient memories was given to England as a thank-offering for her deliverance in the great war of 1914–1918 as a place of rest and recreation for her Prime Ministers for ever."

During the Second World War, Winston Churchill declined to use Chequers as his country retreat due to security concerns, and, when not in London, resided in Ditchley in Oxfordshire until late 1942, when security measures had been put in place. Chequers hosted the leaders of the 24th G8 summit's spouses in 1998, and in 2014, they were visited by Queen Elizabeth II.

What Makes Chequers Very Famous?

Chequers has played host to important political figures and celebrities from all over the world since it became the official country retreat of the Prime Minister in 1921. The family who donated Chequers to the nation, the Lord and Lady of Fareham, recognized the huge political change of the twentieth century and pre-empted a situation where the elected Prime Minister of Great Britain may not have the means to fund his own country house. Chequers is symbolic of Lord and Lady Fareham's vision of a fairer political system, where a lack of wealth or an aristocratic background would not disqualify potential future leaders.

Further Research

- Norma Major and Mark Fiennes (1996) Chequers: The Prime Minister's Country House and its History.
- Gilbert Jenkins (1967) Chequers, A History of the Prime Minister's Buckinghamshire Home

Visiting Information

Chequers is not open to the public.

BRYMPTON D'EVERCY
A Somerset Jewel

Key Facts about the House

- Work on the original Brympton d'Evercy began in the year 1220, although little of the original residence remains.
- Brympton d'Evercy is located on the outskirts of Yeovil in the county of Somerset, England.
- During its 800-year history, Brympton d'Evercy has been owned by just five families.

One of Somerset's most historic houses, Brympton d'Evercy, was once described as 'the most beautiful house in England'. Built slowly over hundreds of years and then refurbished and renovated for every century after, Brympton d'Evercy has evolved slowly and constantly, resulting in a sprawling Grade I listed mansion and estate featuring numerous architectural styles.

The d'Evercy family purchased the estate recorded in the Domesday Book as Brunetone, meaning 'brown enclosure', in 1220, when it was nothing more than a few buildings and a farm. The d'Evercy family added a church, but by the time Brympton d'Evercy passed into the hands of the Sydenham family in 1430, it consisted of a manor house, gardens, two acres of land, and forty house owners. The Sydenhams owned Brympton d'Evercy for the next three hundred years. At one time, the Sydenham family, England's largest landowners, saw their fortunes fluctuate wildly, seeming to rise to prosperity or fall to ruin with each and every generation.

Despite the money troubles that blighted the Sydenham family descendants, many alterations were made to Brympton d'Evercy throughout the 15th, 16th and 17th centuries. As a family of stature, the Sydenhams could not be seen to fall behind the times and their additions to Brympton d'Evercy were heavily influenced by the building works of their Somerset neighbors and new ideas of domestic comfort and privacy.

The first John Sydenham enhanced what is now known as the Priest's House, a small medieval oddity built close to the mansion house. Perhaps it was a guest house or, more likely, it was intended as a dower house for the first Mrs. Sydenham who could not have known that her son would die before her, leaving her to live in the main house for as long as she pleased.

The north wing came next, a turreted, richly ornamented, and quintessentially Tudor affair with large oriel windows and a castellated roof. Almost a house within a house, the north wing has its own external entrance and has changed little since it was built around 1520. Sometimes called the Henry VIII wing, the upper windows of the north wing feature the beautifully sculpted coat of arms of King Henry VIII. The Sydenhams were bestowed with this regal honor due to their, somewhat tenuous, connections to royal blood. The fourth John Sydenham built Brympton d'Evercy's west front around the original great hall and his son, the fifth John Sydenham, built the large, barrel-vaulted roofed kitchen wing.

The last John Sydenham built the entire Palladian-style south wing. Although the architect responsible for the south wing remains a mystery, it is this addition to Brympton d'Evercy that transformed it from a country manor to one of England's great houses. The state apartments located on the ground floor are the most carefully and lavishly decorated in the entire house and consist of the usual arrangement of a salon leading through gradually smaller and more intimate rooms to the state bedroom. No royal ever came to stay at Bryptom d'Evercy and the rooms were soon refashioned into more usable spaces.

By the time the last John Sydenham's son, Philip Sydenham, got hold of the keys to the castle, funds were all but depleted. Philip attempted to sell the Brymtpon d'Evercy estate in 1697 for £16-

20,000 but as no buyer was interested, he mortgaged Brymton d'Evercy to Thomas Penny, the tax collector for Somerset. After making significant alterations to the mansion, Penny fell on his own hard times, losing his job for misappropriation of funds and dying poor in 1731.

Thanks to Penny, Brympton House now has a castellated and glazed porch on its south front, its own clock tower, and a fine new entrance to the Priest tower. Brympton d'Evercy sold at an auction in 1731 to the Fane, and later Ponsonby-Fane, a family whose impact on the estate was negligible but whose impact on easily-scandalized Victorian society was notable. The house was largely empty until John 10th Earl of Westmorland's wife Jane Saunders and her daughter Lady Georgina Fane took up residence. That these ladies lived independently of the Earl was scandalizing enough, but Lady Georgiana's affair with the Duke of Wellington is what really got society talking. The affair never became a marriage and Lady Georgiana lived on at Brympton d'Evercy alone following her mother's death.

By the time the estate passed on to Georgiana's nephew, Spencer Ponsonby, it was heavily in debt and the young man made a reluctant return from Ireland, where he is thought to have been avoiding a court subpoena, to claim his inheritance. One look at Brympton d'Evercy and the prodigal nephew is thought to have turned his life around. Vowing to retain the estate no matter what, Ponsonby became a prominent civil servant, fathered 11 children, and transformed the quiet house into a cricket lover's haven, hosting a house party dedicated to English cricket every year.

Two world wars took their toll on Brympton d'Evercy and upon the death of Violet Clive, sister of owner Richard Ponsonby-Fane, in 1955, the entire contents of Brympton d'Evercy was sold, including the large collection of art and antiques amassed by Lady Georgiana and her mother, the countess of Westmorland. The empty house was used as a public school for the next twenty years. In 1974 Charles Clive-Ponsonby Fane reclaimed Brympton d'Evercy as his home and set about restoring it as a visitor attraction. Unfortunately, it was impossible to replace what had been sold and the enterprise failed. Now Brympton d'Evercy belongs to the Glossop family, who use it as a wedding venue and filming location.

Why is Brympton d'Evercy Famous?

The architecture of Brympton d'Evercy House is as eclectic as the personalities of the many families that have called it home over the last 800 years. Famously named 'the most beautiful house in England' by writer Christopher Hussey, Brympton d'Evercy was built slowly over the course of hundreds of years but fared badly in the 20th century following two world wars and a huge auction that left it almost a shell. Despite these hardships, Brympton d'Evercy is still a family home and still one of England's great houses.

Brympton d'Evercy in TV and Film

- Restoration (1995)
- Middlemarch (1994 mini-series)
- Mansfield Park (1983 mini-series)

Further Research

- Charles Clive-Ponsonby-Fane (1980) Brympton d'Evercy

Visitors' Information

Brympton d'Evercy is privately owned and is not open to the public. It's available to hire out for weddings, however.

BALMORAL CASTLE
The Royal Family's Private Scottish Home

Brief Facts about Balmoral Castle

- Balmoral Castle is located in Royal Deeside, Aberdeenshire, Scotland.
- The current Balmoral Castle was built in 1856.
- The first Balmoral Castle was built in 1390 but was demolished in 1856 once the new castle was complete.
- The Balmoral estate was purchased by Prince Albert, Consort to Queen Victoria, in 1852, and the house and estate remain the private property of the royal family.

Balmoral Castle will forever be known as the happy family home of Queen Victoria, Prince Albert, and their nine children. An epic Scotch Baronial castle fit for the Queen of Great Britain and grandmother of Europe, Balmoral Castle remains the autumnal residence of the Royal family to this day. The family regularly uses it in the summers and when doing official visits in Scotland.

On a flat expanse of meadowland on the south bank of the river Dee, 50 miles west of Aberdeen, sits Balmoral Castle. King Robert II of Scotland was the first monarch to be wooed by this patch of land, having a hunting lodge built here in the 14th century, but is by no means the last as Balmoral has been one of the private residences of the British royal family since 1852.

The first reference to a castle at Balmoral appears in 1452, referred to as 'Bouchmorale.' In 1539, the castle appeared again under the tenancy of Alexander and John Gordon, sons of the 1st Earl of Huntly, who added a tower house to the existing structure.

The castle was inherited by Anne Farquharson, wife of Charles Farquharson, a Jacobite who fought in the battle of Killiecrankie. Following the Battle of Falkirk of 1746, where Farquharson's nephew James earned his name as 'Balmoral the Brave,' the castle was forfeited and bought by the Earl of Fife. The lease next passed to Sir Robert Gordon, brother of the Prime Minister Earl of Aberdeen, who set about adding a major extension to the castle, designed by John Smith of Aberdeen.

One morning, so the story goes, Sir Robert Gordon died suddenly at his breakfast table in Balmoral Castle. At the same time, Queen Victoria, Prince Albert, and their three children were enduring torrential weather in the West highlands. Heeding the royal doctor's advice that Queen Victoria would benefit from the drier and more pleasant climate of Deeside, Prince Albert quickly entered negotiations with the Fife Trustees to take over the lease of Balmoral Castle, complete with its furniture and staff.

The first visit by Queen Victoria and Prince Albert to Balmoral Castle took place in September 1848. Prince Albert decided to purchase Balmoral outright, as well as the neighboring estate of Birkall and the lease of Abergeldie in the name of the Prince of Wales, the future Edward VII, who was seven years old at the time. Balmoral was thus his personal estate and did not come under the administration of the other royal residences.

Victoria and Albert's growing family, along with the administrative and social necessities of a royal household, made it clear that extending the existing castle wouldn't suffice. In 1852, the decision was made to build a brand new castle 100m from the site of the old one. William Smith, City architect of Aberdeen and son of John Smith, who designed the earlier castle, was commissioned to design a new castle that would sit around a central clock tower that would reach a height of 100 feet and would be large enough to house 130 people at a time.

Balmoral Castle has two main blocks, the 'offices' and the royal and guest apartments, both with central courtyards and linked to the tower by two-story wings. Described as a restrained version of 19th century 'Scotch Baronial' architecture, the castle features round towers and turrets and a carriage porch entrance bearing the arms of Prince Albert in marble. Balmoral Castle is made of local grey granite quarried from Invergelder on the estate, and the roofing slates are from Foundland in central Aberdeenshire.

Building work began in 1853; Victoria and Albert moved into the royal apartments in 1855, and by 1856, work was complete, and the old castle was demolished. Up until his sudden death in 1861, Prince Albert had an active role in making various improvements to the estate, rebuilding cottages, creating plantations, improving the approach to Balmoral, and developing a model dairy. Following Albert's death, Queen Victoria continued to visit Balmoral and spent increasing amounts of time there until her own death in 1901. The royal family has continued to use Balmoral Castle for annual autumn visits up to the present day.

Balmoral Castle is a Historic Scotland category A listed building and is located within the Cairngorms National Park. Balmoral working estate includes a grouse moor, farmland, public fishing, and hiking, and managed herds of Highland cattle, deer, and ponies. In 1931, Balmoral Castle was first opened to the public. A visit includes a tour of the largest room in the Castle, the Ballroom, and access to the gardens and exhibitions. There is no access to Balmoral during the months of August, September, and October as the Royal Family is in residence.

What Makes Balmoral Famous?

Balmoral's fame undoubtedly comes from its royal connection. Although still used by the Royal Family during the Autumn months, Balmoral will always be known as the home of Queen Victoria and Prince Albert. The monarchy's purchasing of a Scottish estate and adoption of Scottish architectural style in the mid-19th century went a long way in promoting highland culture to the rest of Scotland and solidifying the relationship between the two largest countries in Great Britain.

Balmoral in TV and Film

Balmoral Estate has been used as a location for the following films and TV shows

- The World from Above (2010) TV Series
- Romeo and Juliet Revisited (2002) Film
- Prince William: A Royal Portrait (1999) Documentary
- The Queen Mother: A Royal Century (1999) Documentary
- Network First: Victoria and Albert (1997) TV Series
- Sixty Glorious Years (1938) Film
- Arrival of Edward II at Balmoral (1901) Documentary
- Review of the Yeoman of the Guard (1899) Documentary
- Review of the Highland Clans (1899) Documentary
- The Highland Reel (1899) Documentary
- The Highland Fling (1899) Documentary
- The Queen and Princess of Battenburg (1899) Documentary

The following films were set at Balmoral Castle, but filming was done elsewhere.

- The Queen (2006) Film
- Mrs Brown (1997) Film

Further Research

- Cuthbert Graham (1972) Portrait of Aberdeen and Deeside
- Newbury, Williams, and Jolles (1984) Balmoral Castle: Great Houses
- Rodney Castleden (2013) The Castles and Britain and Ireland
- David Cook (2000) Castles of Scotland
- Ronald Clarke (2011) Balmoral: Queen Victoria's Highland Home

Visiting information

Balmoral Castle is open to the public from the 1st of April to the 31st of July each year, and opening hours are between 10.00 am and 5.00 pm. For more information, visit the website www.balmoralcastle.com

BLETCHLEY PARK
The House That Cracked Enigma

Key Facts about Bletchley Park

- Bletchley Park is located in Milton Keynes, Buckinghamshire, England.
- The present house was built in 1883 by Sir Herbert Leon.
- The mansion was home to Sir Herbert Leon and his family until 1938, when it became the base for MI6's communications operation.
- Bletchley Park is where Alan Turing and his team broke the German Enigma Code and completed the mathematical work that formed the basis of modern electronic computing.

The name 'Bletchley Park' conjures an image of harassed mathematicians hunched over monstrous typewriters, inputting endless numbers and letters, pale-faced women wired into huge switchboards, listening, and everywhere the pained silence of ultra-secret, life or death, wartime work. Bletchley Park was once simply a curious, Victorian English country home, but today, it is one of the most influential historic sites of World War Two and has benefitted greatly from a recent heritage lottery-funded renovation.

Originally a part of the estate of the Manor of Eaton, the site of Bletchley Park is mentioned in the great Doomsday Book of 1086. A house was built on this historic plot of land in 1711 by a man named Browne Willis. In 1793, the house was demolished, and it wasn't until 1883 that Sir Herbert Leon expanded the remaining farmhouse on the site and built the mansion known as Bletchley Park.

The Bletchley mansion is an unusual and eclectic design that incorporates elements of Victorian Gothic, Dutch Baroque, and Tudor architectural styles. Founded and funded by millionaire Sir Herbert Leon, the mansion's exterior features both Dutch and Tudor gables and a Moorish-influenced roof. The building is asymmetrical in design, with sumptuous interiors featuring reproduction Jacobean ceilings, marble arches, and an impressive ballroom with gilded ceilings.

In May 1938, Bletchley Park went from being a little-known and somewhat curious English country home to being one of the most important centers of British intelligence during the Second World War. Under Sir Richard Gambier-Perry Bletchley Park, the mansion and 38 acres of land were transformed into the headquarters for MI6's communications operation in preparation and anticipation of the outbreak of war with Germany.

Bletchley Park, known as B.P. to those who worked there, was chosen due to its prime location almost immediately adjacent to Bletchley Railway Station, a main road linking London to the North West of England and a telegraph and telephone station at Fenny Stratford. Throughout the Second World War, Bletchley Park was the location of British military intelligence and code-breaking, the most influential example being the cracking of the German Enigma code and the building of the Colossus computer in 1943 to decrypt the Lorenz cipher used by the Nazi high command. MI6 and the GC&CS (Government Code and Cypher School) collected staff from various backgrounds to join the code-breaking efforts at Bletchley Park. The most famous of the 'Code-breakers' were cryptoanalyst Dilly Knox and mathematicians Alan Turing and Peter Twinn.

At the peak of MI6's code-breaking efforts in early 1945, around 9000 people were working at Bletchley. In order to accommodate the many staff and extensive equipment, a large number of buildings were added to those already in existence on the site of Bletchley Park. Wooden huts known by number and brick-built blocks known by letter were built all over the grounds of Bletchley Park to house the many departments, workers, and equipment needed by the code-breaking teams.

Following the Second World War, much of the equipment

and documents held at Bletchley Park were destroyed, and the buildings were left to ruin. The site of Bletchley Park was used as a teacher-training college and local GPO headquarters in the sixties and seventies, but by the 1990s, it was at risk of being demolished to make way for re-development. The Milton Keynes Borough Council stepped in and declared Bletchley Park a conservation area. The Bletchley Park Trust was formed and opened the site to visitors in 1993 as a museum.

Bletchley Park has recently undergone a huge renovation funded by the Heritage Lottery and re-opened to visitors in June 2014, complete with a new visitors' center, renovated huts, and newly landscaped gardens. Bletchley Park's main attractions include the rebuilt Bombe and Enigma machine, which sit alongside Glyn Hughes' full-size sculpture of Alan Turing in Block B, The National Museum of Computing in Block H, the Mansion itself and various displays focused on subjects such as the Home Front, Maritime History, The Diplomatic Wireless Service and Toys and Memorabilia.

What Makes Bletchley Park Famous?

The work of the Code-breakers who toiled at Bletchley Park during the Second World War was considered 'Ultra' secret, even more secret than the 'Most' secret operations, and as such, all workers were sworn to absolute secrecy, a command some Bletchley workers have obeyed right up to this day. A chain of wireless intercept stations around the country collected messages sent by various enemy armies and sent them on to Bletchley Park to be deciphered, translated, and fed back to the British Army in intelligence reports that were used by commanders in the field. Winston Churchill famously described the code-breakers who worked at Bletchley Park as "the geese that laid the golden eggs and never cackled."

Bletchley Park on Film and TV

Bletchley Park was featured as a location in the following

films and TV shows.

- The Imitation Game (2014) Film
- The Bletchley Circle (2012-) TV series
- Danger UXB (1979) TV Series

Further Research

- Aldrich, Richard J. (2010) GCHQ: The Uncensored Story of Britain's Most Secret Intelligence Agency
- Copeland, B. Jack, ed. (2006) Colossus: The Secrets of Bletchley Park's Codebreaking Computers
- See also Timewatch Special 'Codebreakers: Bletchley Park's Lost Heroes' and the 1999 documentary series 'Station X'.
- Gannon, Paul (2011) Inside Room 40: The Codebreakers of World War II
- McKay, Sinclair (2010) The Secret Life of Bletchley Park: The WWII Codebreaking Centre and the Men and Women Who Worked There
- Smith, Michael and Butters, Lindsey (2007) The Secrets of Bletchley Park: Official Souvenir Guide

Visiting Information

Bletchley Park is run by the Bletchley Park Trust and is open to visitors every day except the 24th, 25th, and 26th of December and the 1st of January. During summer, the park is open from 9.30 am to 5 pm, and in winter, it is open from 9.30 am to 4 pm. Visit the website www.bletchleypark.org.uk for more.

WADDESDON MANOR
The House Built by the Rothschild Banking Dynasty

Key Facts about Waddesdon Manor

- Waddesdon Manor is located in the town of Waddesdon in Buckinghamshire, England.
- Waddesdon Manor was built between the years 1874 and 1889 by architect Gabriel-Hippolyte Destailleur for Baron Ferdinand de Rothschild.
- The Manor and its contents were bequeathed to the National Trust in 1957 but still overseen by the Rothschild Trust.

Waddesdon Manor is a Louis XIV-style French Renaissance château lavishly built in the heart of the Buckinghamshire countryside by Baron Ferdinand de Rothschild. As extravagant as you would expect, Waddesdon Manor is one the grandest country houses in the UK and contains an internationally significant collection of 18th-century French furnishings and 18th and 19th-century paintings.

In 1874, at the age of 35, the recently widowed Ferdinand de Rothschild of the Viennese branch bought a plot of land in the Vale of Aylesbury and set about his lifelong mission of building a Louis XIV-style French Renaissance Chateau in the heart of the English Countryside. Rothschild, along with his architect Gabriel-HippolyteDestailleur conceived of a house in the style of the great Renaissance Châteaux of the Loire Valley, a style in which Destailleur had much experience due to his restoration work on many house châteaux in that region.

Internally, the house was designed to utilize the most modern structural design and architectural principles of the time, including a steel framework supporting the upper floors, central heating, and an electric bell system, said to have been coveted by Queen Victoria during her visit in 1890. Externally, Waddesdon Manor was the picture of ornate and opulent French Renaissance style.

Waddesdon features a stunning twin staircase on the north facade, inspired by that of the Chateau de Chambord, and its towers are inspired by those of the Chateau de Maintenon. Visitors approach Waddesdon Manor by ascending a winding, tree-lined driveway that suddenly opens up to view across a beautiful Italian garden to the Manor's spectacular facade complete with pinnacles, turrets, and chimneys unlike any seen in the Buckinghamshire countryside.

The gardens at Waddesdon Manor were designed by French landscape architect Ellie Lane, and, in an extravagant move for the time, many full-grown trees were transplanted around the grounds. Pavillions, statuary, and an aviary were added to the gardens along with the crowning finish of The Proserpina fountain, brought to Waddesdon at the end of the 19th century from the Ducal Palace of Colorno in Italy.

The influence of the most extravagant Frenchman in history, Louis XIV, can be seen in even headier doses within the walls of Waddesdon Manor. The furnishings, fittings, and artwork that fill the many rooms of this epic home make up one of the finest private collections of art and furniture in the UK.

The rooms of Waddesdon Manor were furnished by Baron Ferdinand using his large collection of French 18th-century ceramics, furniture, and tapestries. In the dining room hang 18th century Beauvais tapestries based on the work of Boucher, in the Red Drawing Room sits a chest by the royal cabinet maker Riesener, and in Baron Ferdinand's Room sits a desk once owned by Beaumarchais and a Riesener secretaire.

The Baron's collection of paintings is no less impressive, with portraits by Reynolds and Gainsborough hanging in the Red Drawing Room and work by Dutch masters Hooch, Ruisdael, Cuyp, and Dou hanging in the west wing's morning room. Upstairs, Waddesdon Manor has been partly restored, with half of the space fitted as bedrooms and half of the space converted to exhibition spaces. The bedrooms are exquisitely furnished and feature pieces by Meissen and Boucher.

In 1898, on Baron Ferdinand Rothschild's death, Waddesdon Manor passed to his sister Alice de Rothschild, who had lived with him there for most of her life. After Alice's death in 1922, the manor passed to her nephew James A. Rothschild, a Liberal MP, who added objects and paintings from his late father, Baron Edmond James de Rothschild of Paris's collection, to the already stunning collection at Waddesdon.

On Baron Ferdinand's death, Waddesdon's collection of Renaissance works and arms was bequeathed to the British Museum, and on James Rothschild's death in 1957, he bequeathed the Waddesdon Manor itself and its complete contents to the National Trust to be preserved and conserved for posterity. The property is currently tenanted by the 4th Lord Rothschild, who, in an unprecedented arrangement, was given authority by the National Trust to run Waddesdon Manor as a semi-independent operation. In 2012, Waddesdon Manor was given the honor of being designated one of the sites for Jubilee Woodlands commemorating Queen Elizabeth II's Diamond Jubilee.

Why is Waddesdon Manor Famous Today?

The collection held within the walls of Waddesdon Manor is internationally recognized as one of the most exemplary collections of 18th-century French furnishings and 18th and 19th-century paintings by Flemish, Dutch, and French artists in the world. The magnificent houses built by the Rothschilds and their painstakingly preserved collections became known by their own descriptor, 'gout Rothschild,' and Waddesdon Manor is one of the best examples of that splendor. Waddesdon Manor was featured in the international press in 2003 when The Johnson Gang stole approximately 100 pieces of French snuff boxes and other jeweled objects from the collection that are believed to have belonged to, among others, Marie Antoinette and Madame de Pompadour.

TV and Films Featuring Waddesdon Manor

Waddesdon Manor has been featured in the following films and TV shows.

- Sherlock Holmes: A Game of Shadows (2011) Film
- The Mummy Tomb of the Dragon Emperor (2008) Film
- The Queen (2006) Film
- Downton Abbey (2011) TV Series

Further Research

- Mrs James de Rothschild (1979) Rothschilds at Waddesdon Manor
- Michael Hall and John Bigelow Taylor (2002) Waddesdon Manor: The Heritage of a Rothschild House

Visitor Information

Waddesdon Manor is run by the National Trust and is open to visitors from Wednesday to Sunday from 10.00 am to 5.00 pm. Both the house and gardens are closed on Mondays and Tuesdays. See the website www.Waddesdon.org.uk for more information.

LEEDS CASTLE
"The Loveliest Castle in the World"

Brief Facts about the House

- Leeds Castle is five miles southeast of Maidstone in Kent, England.
- The castle was first built on this site in 1119 by Robert de Crevecour.
- The castle today dates mainly from the 19th
- Leeds Castle has belonged to a private charitable trust, Leeds Castle Foundation, since 1976.
- Not located anywhere near Leeds the city.

You can't talk about the history of the English royal family in medieval times without taking a moment to acknowledge Leeds Castle. First, a Norman stronghold, Leeds Castle has been the royal residence of six queens of Medieval Britain, and if walls could talk, I'm sure it would have some secrets to tell. Now a 19th-century gothic castle built amongst 12th-century ruins, Leeds Castle is known as the 'loveliest castle in the world.'

Built as a Norman stronghold in the years following the Norman Conquest, the first stone castle to be built on the site of Leeds Castle was owned by the de Crevecour family until around 1260. From 1276 and throughout most of the Middle Ages, the crown owned the castle. Leeds Castle was first owned by King Edward 1st, who made a gift of it to his Queen, Eleanor of Castile. Edward enhanced and improved the castle, adding a Barbican on the outermost island accessible by three causeways, each defended by its drawbridge, gateway, and portcullis, and a Gloriette on the smallest island with apartments for the King and Queen. It is thought that the artificial lake surrounding the three islands castle was also added at this time.

Many famous historical events happened within and just outside the walls of this castle. In 1321, Edward II besieged Leeds Castle after Baroness Badlesmere, wife of the constable of the castle, refused entry to the King's consort Isabella of France and ordered her archers to fire upon her party. Six people were killed, and Baroness Badlesmere was imprisoned in the Tower of London for one year as punishment. The castle moved through the hands of Edward II's widow, Isabella of France, her son Edward III, and his grandson Richard II before being granted to Richard's wife, Anne of Bohemia, in 1382. Richard's successor gave Leeds Castle to his wife, Joan of Navarre, who passed it down to Henry V, who then bequeathed it to his wife, Catherine de Valois.

Perhaps the most famous of Leeds Castle's owners was King Henry VIII, who transformed Leeds Castle into a palace for his first wife, Catherine of Aragon, in 1519, adding, amongst other things, a maiden tower to house the Queen's Maids of Honour. Amongst these maids was Anne Boleyn, Henry VIII's second wife and mother of Elizabeth I, who was imprisoned in Leeds Castle before her coronation. The castle was a Parliamentarian arsenal and prison during the Civil War and escaped destruction. The castle fell into ruin in succeeding years until, in 1820, it was repaired and remodeled by the current owners, the Wykeham-Martin family.

The Wykeham-Martins built a gothic-style house on the main island of the castle and rebuilt the Gloriette, which had been damaged in a fire. Various medieval outbuildings have survived, as has Catherine of Aragon's maiden tower. Past the mock medieval New Castle is the Gloriette, complete with an internal timbered Fountain Court, thought to have been rebuilt by the Wykeham-Martins. The corridors of the Gloriette lead to the banqueting hall, chapel, staterooms, and Queen's gallery.

In the 1920s, Leeds castle was bought by Lady Baillie, an Anglo-American and beneficiary of the Whitney millions, who completely redecorated the interior, restoring many of the rooms to their previous medieval splendor. Working with French architect Armand-Albert Rateau, Lady Baillie completely rebuilt the interior of the New Castle, adding a 16th-century style wooden staircase, a drawing room removed in full from Thorpe Hall, and a 17th-century French-styled library and dining room, the latter of which was designed to display 18th century Aubusson tapestries. Both the Queen's bedroom and Gallery were restored to look as they did in the fifteenth century during the reign of Henry V and Queen Catherine and are fully furnished with antiques.

Following Lady Baillie's death in 1974, Leeds Castle was bequeathed to the Leeds Castle Foundation, a charitable trust that opened the castle to the public in 1976 and has looked after it ever since. To encourage tourism, an aviary was added to Leeds Castle in 1980 but closed for financial reasons in 2012, and in 1988, a maze was added to the gardens of the castle. Leeds Castle is a Grade I listed historical building and one of the most visited heritage attractions in the UK.

What Makes Leeds Castle Famous

With foundations reaching back to the year 857AD, Leeds Castle is mentioned in the Domesday Book and was once a Norman Stronghold. A royal residence for many years, the sheer number of kings and queens who have resided in Leeds Castle over the years guarantees its fame. Once known as the 'ladies' castle,' Leeds was the Royal residence of six Queens of Medieval Britain, bearing witness to all of the trials and tribulations of each of their time on the throne. Thanks to its spectacular setting on three islands surrounded by a beautiful artificial lake, Leeds Castle has become known today as 'the loveliest castle in the world.'

Leeds Castle in Film and TV

Leeds Castle has featured as a location in the following films and TV shows

- Elizabeth – The Golden Age (2007) Film
- Elizabeth (1998) Film

- Lady Jane (1986) Film
- Dr Who (1963) TV Series
- Waltz of the Toreadors (1962) Film
- Moonraker (1958) Film
- Kind Hearts and Coronets (1949) Film
- If Winter Comes (1923) Film

Further Research

- Nick McCann (2000) 'Leeds Castle – Great Houses of Britain'
- Scala Publishing (2010) 'Leeds Castle: Queen of Castles, Castle of Queens'
- Anthony Russel (2013) 'Outrageous Fortune: Growing Up in Leeds Castle'

Visiting Information

Leeds Castle is run by the charitable trust 'Leeds Castle Foundation' and is open to the public all year round. Opening times are from 10.30 am to 6.00 pm during the summer and 10.30 am to 5.00 pm during the winter. For more information, visit the website www.leeds-castle.com.

Getting there – by road

Located 7 miles east of Maidstone, Junction 8 of the M20 motorway is just 1 hour from London and 30 minutes from the Channel Tunnel and Channel Ports. Dartford River Crossing 30 minutes. Clearly, signs were posted from all routes – following the brown and white tourist signs.

Getting there – by rail

They recommend travelling to Bearsted Station. Southeastern runs frequent services to and from Bearsted, and a coach shuttle service run by Spot Travel is available from the station from April to September. A private service is also available from October to March.

CHARTWELL
The Beloved Home of Sir Winston Churchill

Key Facts about Chartwell

- Chartwell is located two miles from the town of Westerham in Kent, England.
- The first house built on this site dates to the 16th
- Chartwell belonged to Sir Winston Churchill and was his family home from 1924 until his death.

Chartwell, the family home of Sir Winston Churchill for most of his adult life, is a museum and shrine to the man who led Great Britain to victory during the Second World War. Now a National Trust property, Chartwell is an understated Victorian country house, originally dating from Tudor times, with beautiful gardens and a spectacular view of the Weald of Kent that Churchill is said to have loved. He customized the house to his specifications over the years, creating a sanctum where he did his most productive writing.

Over 700 years before its most famous resident, Sir Winston Churchill, stepped through the door of Chartwell House, someone else was calling it home. Local records suggest that there was a property built on this site as early as 1362, and the name Chartwell was most likely derived from the chart (Kentish for common) well that lies on the site and still feeds the ponds to the north of the house to this day.

The Chartwell House you can visit today was built during Tudor times, and analysis of the wood dates the building to between 1515 and 1546. The house was probably built as a hunting lodge and has spectacular views over a lake and private valley with the Wealden Hills rolling out into the distance. It is thought that King Henry VIII stayed there while courting Anne Boleyn, who was living at nearby Hever Castle.

The property became known as 'Well Street' in the late 1700s and was used as a foundling house as part of the London Foundling Hospital until 1836 when it was sold to the Drinkwater Bethune family from Surrey. The next owners, the Campbell Colquhouns, renamed the house Chartwell and made huge developments and alterations to the house and land before it was purchased by Winston Churchill in 1922. A dark, red-brick, ivy-clad villa on a hill, Chartwell was said to embody Victorian architecture at its least attractive. Churchill set about remodeling and extending the house straight away, enlisting the help of a young architect, Philip Tilden.

For the next two years, Tilden transformed the house, adding larger windows to let in more light and more rooms, retaining period features such as stepped gables and warm pink brickwork but erasing any Tudor revivalist influences. Despite two years of renovation work, Churchill's Chartwell was a modestly comfortable, almost suburban home without any of the grandeur one might expect from the home of a victorious wartime prime minister.

Chartwell's position so close to the English Channel made it vulnerable during World War II, so during this time, the Churchills resided mainly at Ditchley, Oxfordshire, and later at the official country residence of the Prime Minister at Chequers, Buckinghamshire,

It's no secret that Churchill's financial situation was often unstable, and in 1938, Churchill was almost forced to sell Chartwell for financial reasons. At the time, the house was advertised as featuring five reception rooms, nineteen beds and dressing rooms, eight bathrooms, and eighty acres of land. Wealthy friends of Churchill bought Chartwell for the National Trust in 1946 on the condition that Churchill and his family could live there until their deaths. It was presented to the public in 1966, one year after Churchill's death.

Chartwell today is a monument to Churchill's life, and his

presence fills every inch of the house. Visitors can walk through Churchill's famous front door with its striking 18th-century surroundings and wander through the rooms of his house. Churchill's study is the heart of Chartwell, and most evoke the Tudor origins of the property with old roof timbers, a Tudor doorway, and views of the valley. Churchill spent most of his time in this room after his retirement, sleeping in a four-poster bed in the corner in order to return to work as soon as he woke.

The house is crammed with memorabilia from Churchill's life, and the walls are lined with photographs of the famous faces Churchill met during his time as prime minister and into his retirement. While much of Chartwell is shrine-like, each room a museum exhibition of Churchill's incredible legacy, there are traces of the real-life lived within its walls. Churchill's wife Clementine's beloved Rose Garden, the dining room where Churchill used to show after-dinner films, and, of course, Churchill's art studio offer a little more than typical house museums can.

Churchill's love of painting was a huge part of his life and provided some relief from the periodic bouts of depression he famously referred to as his 'black dog.' In the 1930s, Churchill converted a cottage on the property into an art studio and, throughout the rest of his lifetime, completed up to 500 paintings, many of which are now owned by universities, museums, and private collectors. Our current monarch, Queen Elizabeth II, has one of Churchill's paintings in her private collection. Around 130 of Churchill's paintings, often described as Impressionist in style, hung on the various walls of Chartwell, and Churchill's beloved studio has been left just as he left it, with an easel and palette in place.

A cozy family home, Chartwell is not designed for coach loads of visitors, and the usual car park and visitor center you would expect from a National Trust property are located on a hillside at a distance from the house. A typical visit includes a tour of the house, entry to temporary exhibitions, and a tour of the gardens.

What Makes Chartwell Famous?

Chartwell is famous for the sole reason that Sir Winston Churchill, Prime Minister of the United Kingdom during the Second World War, lived there for most of his adult life. The house has been preserved exactly as it was when Churchill lived there as a shrine to the man, his life, and his legacy. It's not a particularly grand country house, but it qualifies as a Great British House purely because of its connection to Churchill.

Anglotopia's Take

Anyone interested in Churchill or World War II history must visit Chartwell at least once. It is a beautiful and intimate place where you can really get a sense of the man behind the legend. It's a very personal place. It was his home. But it was also a place of work for his writing but also when he was a politician. He shaped the landscape to his will and set up the entire household and ground to cultivate his own interests. Don't miss out on visiting his painting studio, where there are dozens of his beautiful paintings to view.

Chartwell in Film and TV

- The Gathering Storm (2002) TV Movie
- A History of Britain (2000) TV Series
- Churchill – The Wilderness Years TV mini Series
- Young Winston (1972) Film

Further Research

- Mary Soames (1992) Chartwell Guide Book
- Roy Jenkins (2002) Churchill: A Biography
- Stefan Buczacki (2007) Churchill and Chartwell: The Untold Story of Churchill's Houses and Gardens
- Chartwell, Kent by the National Trust (2010)

Visiting Information

From the beginning of March until the end of October, Chartwell is open to visitors from 11 am to 4.15 pm every day. Cheaper tickets are available for access to the garden and studio only. See the website www.nationaltrust.org.uk/chartwell for more information. It's pretty easy to get there from London, but it requires a train trip. We recommend taking a train to Sevenoaks station (6 miles away) as it has a regular fast train service from London Charing Cross, Waterloo East, and London Bridge, and there are ample taxis waiting outside the station when you arrive. Grab a taxi and have them take you to Chartwell. If you have time, Hever Castle is also nearby and worth a visit. The Taxi driver will be happy to wait for you or return at a scheduled time.

OSBORNE HOUSE
Queen Victoria's Great Seaside Retreat

Key Facts about Osborne House

- Owned by Queen Victoria and Prince Albert
- The location of Queen Victoria's death
- A renowned military retirement home

Osborne House, located on the Isle of Wight, is an architectural marvel that has captivated the hearts of many visitors over the years. Built in the 19th century as a summer residence for Queen Victoria and her family, the house boasts a rich history that spans several decades. With its impressive Italian Renaissance architecture, opulent furnishings, and stunning gardens, Osborne House has become a symbol of British heritage and a popular tourist destination for history buffs and architecture enthusiasts alike.

There is very little known about the first Osborne house that was present when the property was purchased by the royal family. What is known is that the estate was owned by the Blachford family in 1705. From 1774 to 1781, Robert Pope Blachford commissioned the building of a three-story residence with a stable block and a walled kitchen garden.

To escape the pressure of royalty, Queen Victoria and Prince Albert were in the process of shopping for a seaside retreat in 1843.

At the time, Lady Isabella Blachford was the current owner of the Osborne estate, which was recommended to the royal couple by Sir Robert Peel, the Prime Minister. Initially, the estate was acquired by the couple on a lease basis and was later purchased in May 1845 for £28,000.

The current house on the property was much too small for Queen Victoria and Prince Albert. However, they were concerned about restrictions placed by the Department of Woods and Forests. At the time, the department was in charge of government building. Instead, Albert commissioned the help of Thomas Cubitt, who was a skilled master builder. He was also responsible for much of the Duke of Westminster's Belgravia estate in London. Cubitt's recommendation was that instead of adding on to the old house, it was best to build a completely new structure.

The first phase of the building process was the Pavilion in 1846. This was the location for the private quarters of Queen Victoria and Prince Albert, as well as the royal nursery. The next state completed was the household wing, which was the location for accommodations for members of the royal household who traveled with the royal couple. This was finished in 1848. The main wing of the house was built on the site of the old house in 1851. It was connected to the household wing with a long hallway or corridor.

Other building projects that were overseen by Cubitt include estate cottages, a landing house for the coastguard, and a dormitory for the male servants. A sea wall was also added along the coastal side of the estate to protect the house from the natural elements. The main wing of the house was used by the children until 1853, when a Swiss cottage was built for the royal children. It was located a mile east of the house. A stable that was capable of housing 50 horses and carriages was built in 1860. The old stable location present at the time of the purchase was converted into a kitchen with accommodation for the servants. By 1864, formal gardens had been created around the house, as well as driveways that were 21 miles in length.

The final addition of the house was a wing added between 1890 and 1891. This contained the Durbar Room, which was named after the Hindi term for 'court.' It was built for business functions or state meetings. The wing was designed and decorated by Bhai Ram Singh. It now contains engraved silver and copper vases, Indian armor, and a model of an Indian palace that was gifted to Queen Victoria. The Durbar Room was on the ground floor, and the first floor was created for the Queen's youngest daughter, Beatrice. She was very close to her mother up until the Queen's death.

In January 1901, Queen Victoria died at Osborne House. Her wish was for the estate to remain in the family. However, her children were not as fond of the seaside house as she was. When no one wanted to claim the ownership of the estate, it was given to the state. The late Queen's bedroom, which was located on the upper floors of the pavilion, was turned into a memorial that was accessible only by the royal family. Osborne House was utilized as a navy school from 1903 to 1921.

Today, Osbourne House is managed by English Heritage and is open to the public. In 2004, the cricket pavilion utilized by the former Naval college was converted into a holiday cottage that is available for public use. Any guests who stay at the cottage are given the right to use the private beach at Osbourne House.

What Makes This House Famous

With the advent of WWI, many large estates and mansions opened their houses to the injured officers of war. The secondary wings of Osborne House were used as a convalescent home during this time period. Two famous patients who lived in the home include A.A. Milne and Robert Graves. The home continued through the mid-1900s and was titled the King Edward VII Retirement Home for Officers. By then, the home had opened its doors to expanded military personnel, such as anyone with a civil service background.

TV & Film Appearances

There are a handful of different TV productions created at Osborne House. These include Treasure Hunt (1982 TV Series), Victoria and Albert Mini-Series (1997), A History of Britain TV series

(2000), and The Victorians TV series (2009). There are currently no film productions that have been created at Osborne House.

Further Research

Hidden in the woods near Osborne House is the Swiss Cottage, which is another museum in itself. It is a detached structure with two levels in a wooden chalet style. It was built between May 1853 and May 1854 for the royal children. Prince Albert commissioned the structure to be built to help his children learn how to become successful adults and, eventually, skillful rulers. It is said that the children escaped to the cottage as much as possible when vacationing at Osborne House. Later, they brought their own children back to the cottage. The royal children loved collecting and exploring. So much so that a separate museum was built near the cottage to display the children's findings. The museum is still present today and contains items such as the first transatlantic telegraph message and a 5-legged deer.

Visiting Information

Osborne House is located on the Isle of Wight, which is not connected to the British mainland (there is no bridge). Ferry Rides are available from easily accessible Portsmouth and take less than an hour. Typically, the house is open Monday to Sunday during the months of April through to the 30th of September. During the colder months, such as November through to February, the grounds are closed during the week and open on the weekend. To find out more information about annual visitor rates, regular admission prices, and opening times, refer to the website at www.english-heritage.org.uk/daysout/properties/osborne.

HEVER CASTLE
The Childhood Home of Anne Boleyn

Key Facts about Hever Castle

- Childhood home of Anne Boleyn
- The gardens were awarded the winner of the most romantic garden award by Gardeners' World Magazine
- The estate has an 18-bedroom, 4-star luxury accommodation suite located in the Astor Wing of the castle to allow guests the opportunity to live as royals for the night.

Hever Castle is a significant historical landmark located in the village of Hever in Kent, England. The castle is best known for being the childhood home of Anne Boleyn, the second wife of King Henry VIII, who played a crucial role in English history. Today, Hever Castle is a popular tourist destination, attracting visitors from all over the world who come to explore its rich history, stunning architecture, and beautiful gardens. The castle is a testament to the wealth and power of the Tudor dynasty and a must-see destination for anyone interested in British history.

Hever Castle was inherited by Thomas Boleyn in 1505. He was born in the castle in 1477 and later inherited the property when his father, Sir William Boleyn, died. Thomas was most famous due to the life of his daughter, Anne Boleyn. She spent much of her early life at Hever Castle before going to court during the reign of King Henry VIII. She later became his mistress and then eventually Queen. It is unknown if Anne was born at Hever. The year of her birth is not recorded. However, she did live at Hever until she was

sent to the Netherlands in 1513 to be educated at the court of the Archduchess Margaret.

The king married four more women after Anne's death, among them Jane Seymour and Anne of Cleves. Jane died twelve days after giving birth to Henry's only heir, Edward. His marriage to Anne of Cleves was short-lived and declared annulled due to its never being consummated. As part of the divorce settlement, she was given Hever Castle. Anne of Cleves died in 1557. At this time, Sir Edward Waldegrave was appointed the task of seizing any properties that had been taken by the Crown. He took over the Hever Castle property and deeded the estate to himself. Unfortunately, the Waldegraves were in favor of Mary I. When Queen Elizabeth I took the throne in 1558, Edward was deprived of his Court duties. He retired to the Hever Castle estate and began improvements on the Castle.

This famous castle has a total of three different construction periods. The first part dates back to 1270 and was comprised of a gatehouse and a walled bailey. These features made the structure a prime medieval defense Castle. The second period of construction was the renovation period. The castle was in major need of repairs and was finally converted into an appropriate manor in 1462. The reconstruction process was ordered by Geoffrey Boleyn, Thomas Boleyn's younger brother and Anne's uncle. He also added a Tudor dwelling to the Castle. The third and last period of renovation occurred in the 20th century when the property was owned by William Waldorf Astor.

After the Waldegraves were no longer inhabitants, but before the 20th century, there were multiple owners of the estate. This left the Castle in ruins. However, in 1749, the Meade Waldo family took over the ownership. They did not reside in the house. Instead, they lived close by at Stonewall Park. They left the Castle to a family of tenant farmers. The residents lived in one section of the house and allowed the public to view historic parts of the house on particular days of the week.

American Ambassador William Waldorf Astor purchased the estate in 1903. Due to the large sum of money that Astor inherited at the time of his father's death in 1890, he was titled as the richest man in America. However, his passion for life was in Europe. He was very disgruntled with America and claimed that it was no place for a gentleman to live. Hever Castle remained in the Astor family until 1983, when it was sold to Mr. John Guthrie, owner of Broadland Properties Ltd.

What Makes This House Famous

Almost every history fan is aware of the Boleyn legacy. The Hever Castle is marketed to the public as being the childhood home of Anne Boleyn. Fans come from all over the world to see this famous house as well as the artifacts that are contained inside. Prior to the marriage of Anne and King Henry, he would visit Anne at the Bolingbroke Castle located near Hever to conduct his courtship. There is still one of Henry's private locks located at Hever Castle. It was taken with him when he visited various noblemen's houses. He fitted this to every door for his security.

On 1 June 1533, Anne was crowned Queen in Westminster Abbey by Archbishop Cranmer. At this time, Anne was pregnant. Everyone was excited and expecting a male heir to carry on the King's legacy. However, in September, when Anne gave birth, it was to a baby girl. She later became Queen Elizabeth I and carried just as much power as the male kings who served on the throne before her. Anne was executed on 19 May 1536 for charges of witchcraft, adultery, incest, and treason.

TV & Film Appearances

Other than the annual film festival that is hosted at the castle grounds every summer, numerous well-known films have been created at Hever Castle. Popular names include Anne of the Thousand Days (1969), Lady Jane (1986), The Princess Bride (1987), King Ralph (1991), Bargain Hunt TV series (2000), Inkheart (2008), and many more popular titles.

Anglotopia's Take

If you visit one Tudor property in Britain, visit Hever Castle. There is so much history to take a look at - with many unique artifacts from the reign of Henry VIII. The American connections are also interesting, and it's fascinating to learn about the restorations that the Astors made to the house. The gardens, while having nothing to do with the Tudor history, are incredible and worth exploring on their own. The Astors built a stunning sculpture collection and have it brilliantly on display.

Further Research

- "Hever Castle: The Story of Anne Boleyn's House" by David Starkey
- "Hever Castle: The History and Architecture of the Childhood Home of Anne Boleyn" by John Martin Robinson
- "Hever Castle and Its Owners" by William Lazenby
- "Anne Boleyn's Hever Castle: A Guide Book" by Owen Emmerson
- "Hever Castle: A Short History and Guide" by John Guy
- "Hever Castle: A Kentish Castle Through the Ages" by James Wright
- "Hever Castle: The Home of Anne Boleyn" by Rosemary Baird
- "The Gardens at Hever Castle" by Neil Miller.

Visiting Information

Hever Castle is open daily but check for closures, as hours can vary with the season. Parking is free for visitors, and annual passes are also available for frequent visitors. Complete information on admission fees, directions, and detailed opening and closing times can be seen at www.hevercastle.co.uk.

LYME PARK
Made Famous as Pemberley in Pride & Prejudice

Key Facts about Lyme Park

- The largest house in Cheshire
- Designated as a Grade I listed building according to English Heritage, meaning that it has the highest architectural characteristics
- The Lyme Caxton Missal is on display in the house library.

Lyme Park is known for its intricate architecture, rich history, and highly sought-after collectibles. The estate is currently managed by the National Trust and is surrounded by beautiful gardens and a deer park. Lyme Park was once the residence of the Legh family, who were known for their contributions to the cultural and political landscape of England. The estate gained further recognition when it was used as a filming location for the 1995 television adaptation of Jane Austen's Pride and Prejudice, where it was featured as Mr. Darcy's residence, Pemberley.

The first owner of the estate was Sir Thomas Danyers in 1346. It was gifted to him by Edward III as a thank-you for his service to the Black Prince in the Battle of Crécy. When Sir Thomas died, the estate was passed on to his daughter, Margaret. She married Piers Legh I, who started the Leghs of Lyme dynasty in 1388. Richard II is said to have taken favor in Piers and, in 1397, granted his family a coat of arms. Unfortunately, two years later, Piers was executed by

Richard's rival, Henry Bolingbroke.

The house that was inherited by Margaret was demolished by Piers Legh VII, and new construction began during the mid-16th century. The designer of the house is unknown. According to original documents, it was an L-shaped house with east and north ranges. During the 1720s, Giacomo Leoni was commissioned to make specific modifications to the house, including the addition of Elizabethan characteristics such as the courtyard and south range. It is somewhat difficult to distinguish which work was Leoni's due to the fact that it contained both Baroque and Palladian styles. The furniture that is presently in the house today was purchased in the 18th century by Piers Legh XIII.

By the early 19th century, the house had begun to deteriorate. During this time, Thomas Legh was the estate owner. He commissioned Lewis Wyatt to help restore and modernize the house between 1816 and 1822. Most of Wyatt's improvements were on the inside of the house, where he redesigned every room. Additional improvements made by Wyatt included a tower structure that provided bedrooms for the servants. He also added an extra wing to the east side of the house that made way for a dining room. Years later, the inheritor William Legh, 1st Baron Newton, added other buildings, such as stables, and he also created the Dutch Garden. Extra improvements were made to the garden during the early 20th century by the 2nd Baron Newton and his wife. It was the 3rd Baron Newton who gave Lyme Park to the National Trust in 1946.

The house measures 190 feet by 130 feet, surrounds a courtyard, and is recorded as the largest house in Cheshire. The older part of the house is built with coarse sandstone, while the newer construction was completed with ashlar sandstone. The entire roof of the house is covered in Welsh slates. When standing in front of the north side, the viewer is shown an arched doorway that has Doric columns on each side. As normal with many stately houses, the ground floor is more rustic, while the upper flooring is smooth to the touch.

In the Entrance Hall of the estate, visitors can get a first-hand look at valuable tapestries that were woven between 1623 and

1636. They were moved to Lyme in 1903 from the Legh's London home. To help accommodate for the placement of the tapestries, the interior decorator at the time, Amadee Joubert, was forced to make alterations, which included removing a tabernacle and demolishing four pilasters. To the east of the Entrance Hall is Wyatt's Dining Room, which is prominent with a stucco ceiling suitable for the time period in which it was created. The overall decoration of the room is reportedly that of an early appearance of the Renaissance Style.

North of the Entrance Hall are two rooms that are elaborately decorated in Elizabethan style: the Drawing Room and the Stag Parlour. Over the fireplace mantel in the Drawing Room is a pair of atlantes and caryatids that frame Elizabeth I's arms. The stained glass windows in this particular room were removed from Lyme Hall and then placed in Disley Church. They were then returned back to Lyme in 1835. In the Stag Parlour, a chimneypiece is prominent over the fireplace, which depicts an Elizabethan house, as well as a hunting scene and the arms of James I. Other rooms of the house that possess an Elizabethan flair include the Stone Parlour, which is located on the ground floor, and the Long Gallery, located on the top floor of the east wing.

The gardens at Lyme Park have been etched out of the land over the course of 600 years. They are situated 270m above sea level and measure up to 17 acres. There are also ponds that surround the gardens, as well as a central fountain, orangery, and exquisite rose gardens. One structure that stands out from the rest, with the exception of the house, is a large tower called the Cage. It stands proudly on a hill to the east of the road visitors utilize for entry to the house. At one time, it was used as a hunting lodge and was later converted into a groundskeeper's cottage. In the early centuries, it was also used to lock up prisoners. A structure was built on the site of the Cage prior to the now-standing structure, but it was taken down around 1580. The new structure was built in 1737. Other structures built on the grounds include Paddock Cottage and Lantern Wood.

What Makes This House Famous

Lyme Park is most commonly known for housing the Lyme Caxton Missal. This is an early printed book that contains the liturgy of the mass, published in 1487 by William Caxton. The copy that is on display in the Library at Lyme Park is the only surviving copy of that particular edition in almost complete condition. To help guests interact with this ancient book, the park has established an interactive audio-visual program that utilizes a touchscreen prompt. Through this system, visitors can make the pages of the book "turn" and hear chants from the missal as they would have been sung 500 years ago.

TV & Film Appearances

The Lyme Park grounds and the house have been used in several different film and TV productions. In the 1995 BBC adaptation of 'Pride and Prejudice,' the exterior was utilized as Pemberley, which was Mr. Darcy's home. It was also utilized as a location for an episode of 'Red Dwarf' and as a center stage for the 2011 film 'The Awakening.'

Further Research

- Lyme Park: A Brief History and Guide by National Trust
- Lyme Park: The House and Garden by Anthony Burton
- The Lyme Park Story by David A. H. Bownes
- Lyme Park: The Garden Guide by National Trust
- The History of Lyme Park by National Trust
- Lyme Park: A History and Guide by Anthony Burton
- The Lyme Park Collection by National Trust
- Lyme Park: A Walk Through History by National Trust
- Lyme Park: The House, Garden and Park by National Trust
- Lyme Park: An Illustrated Guide by National Trust.

Visiting Information

Lyme Park hosts many events each year to connect with their visitors and to bring more families to the park. With a 1,400-acre deer park, there are many outdoor areas to be appreciated. The park currently hosts a jogging group that meets on Thursdays and Wednesdays. They also have fun activities for kids to enjoy that help them connect with nature. Dogs are also welcome on the second weekend of each month from June to October. Other fun attractions include a cellar restaurant and a coffee shop that creates mince pies.

Lyme Park is open at various times throughout the year. It is recommended that you refer to their website for a detailed list of opening and closing times, as well as the cost of admission. Visit the Lyme Park website at www.nationaltrust.org.uk/lyme-park.

WOBURN ABBEY
The Seat of the Bedfords

Key Facts about Woburn Abbey

- John Adams, the second President of the United States, visited Woburn Abbey in 1786
- The house was opened to the public in 1955
- The wife of the 7th Duke of Woburn Abbey, Duchess Anna Maria, is reportedly responsible for making 'Afternoon Tea' an addition to daily English life when she entertained her friends with this popular activity.

Woburn Abbey is one of the many jewels in the crown of England's stately homes. It occupies the east end of the village of Woburn, Bedfordshire, and is the current home of the Duke of Bedford. It is a unique estate that is surrounded by a visitor center, Centre Parcs village, a safari park, and a miniature railway system. There are definitely features that will entice a variety of different cultures and backgrounds.

The original Woburn Abbey was created and founded as a Cistercian abbey in 1145 by Hugh de Bolebec. However, in 1547, it was taken over by Henry VIII. The estate was then given to John Russell, the 1st Earl of Bedford, as a gift from Edward VI for his service to Henry VIII. John became Baron Russell and was created as the 1st Earl of Bedford in 1550. The Russell family actually dates back to the late 1300s, when John's great-great-grandfather, Stephen, represented Weymouth in Parliament.

Francis Russell, the 4th Earl, who is also the grandson of

John, moved his family into Woburn Abbey in the 1620s. By the mid-1630s, Francis had built a two-story wing on the north side of the house, as well as a grotto. Both of these additions are still a part of the house today. The Abbey underwent a major renovation in 1747 when Francis commissioned the services of architects Henry Flitcroft and Henry Holland.

Flitcroft was in charge of designing the elaborate State Apartments, which are located in the front portion of the West Wing. He also designed an impressive Grand staircase, which features an exquisite wrought iron balustrade. To give the impression of height, the stairs are cantilevered from the walls, and the stairs are narrowed towards the top so that they become a single lane with enough room for only one person. Flitcroft was also commissioned to design the Stable blocks present on the grounds, which are referred to as North Court and South Court. They were built around 1750, shortly after the completion of the house construction.

While Flitcroft was responsible for the north portion of the house, Holland was in charge of modernizing the Abbey, as well as redesigning the South side of the building. He completely redesigned the front side of the south wing so that it included a three-part library, which was divided by columns. He also designed the Chinese Dairy, which is located in the gardens, and a large indoor riding school. Holland designed a tennis court that was located behind the Stable Courts. However, the structure was demolished in the 1950s due to damages from dry rot. The library, which is referred to as the Holland Library and Book Room today, contains a variety of collections, including botanical and ornithological books. Many of these are displayed in the book room, as well as a large life-size copy of 'Birds of America' by John James Audubon.

Another architect who was commissioned during the time of the 4th Duke was Sir William Chambers. He was later known as the most prominent architect of the neo-classical era. He was most popular for his Palladian creations, which had extra touches of French, Oriental, and Italian characteristics. He was employed by the Duke to make occasional alterations and was also in charge of building the Chambers Bridge, which separates the Basin Pond from the New Pond. It was constructed around 1770 and contained three semi-circular arches. The architect of the 6th Duke was Sir Jeffry Wyatville. He commissioned his services at the Abbey in 1816 to design the Holland Conservatory for his large sculpture collection. He also constructed the Camellia House in 1822, which is bordered by the East End of the Sculpture Gallery.

After WWII, dry rot was found at the house, and half of the Abbey had to be demolished. After the death of the 12th Duke in 1953, his son, who became the 13th Duke, was fined heavy death duties. Instead of handing over the estate to the National Trust, he pushed through the financial trouble and opened the Abbey to the public in 1955. As other entertainment was added, such as the Safari Park in 1970, the popularity of the Abbey grew as well. When inquired as to how the Duke felt about the negative comments made about his choice to add a safari park, he stated that he would rather be looked down on than be overlooked. He later moved to Monte Carlo in 1975 and left the Abbey to his son, Robin.

The Marquess of Tavistock became the 14th Duke when his father died in November 2002. However, he carried the briefest title as Duke in Russell's history when he died in June 2003. His son, Andrew, now the 15th Duke, continues to run the Woburn Abbey estate with his family. The building is currently listed as a Grade 1 structure, which is the highest category of architecture in England.

What Makes This House Famous

Although the Abbey was visited by many dignitaries over the years, a royal visit by Queen Victoria and Prince Albert in 1841 made a huge impact on the house. Ever since her visit, the room has been properly titled as Queen Victoria's Bedroom. Another event that changed the Abbey in a unique way was WWI. During this time period, Mary, the wife of the 11th Duke, took on the role of a nurse and administrator by establishing a military hospital in the riding school at Woburn Abbey. Years later, Mary, who became known as 'The Flying Duchess,' disappeared on a solo flight to Norfolk in 1937.

The late 14th Duke of Bedford suffered a terrible stroke in 1988. He survived, thanks to highly skilled surgeons. However, for many months, he suffered a disturbance in his speech, which is also known as Aphasia. With the aid of intensive speech therapy, he began to recover. However, he always experienced difficulty in forming words and accessing the dialect he needed to use. Due to his experience, he realized the lack of help for sufferers of Aphasia. To help provide others who experienced his own speech problems with support, he developed and founded the Tavistock Trust. The goal is to ensure that more people have access to support and treatment for Aphasia.

TV & Film Appearances

While many of the film productions that utilized the Abbey as a location occurred years ago, they are still very important in history. In 1970, 'A Lizard in a Woman's Skin' by Lucio Fulci was filmed at the Abbey. Three years later, the estate was used for scenes in 'Coronation Street.' The 13th Duke made a cameo in the movie by playing himself. Neil Diamond held many concerts on the front lawn of the Abbey in both 1977 and 2003. The concerts in 1977 were filmed and broadcast on national television in the United States.

Further Research

- Woburn Abbey: The Park & Gardens by Keir Davidson
- A Guide to Woburn Abbey by J. D. (John Docwra)

Visiting Information

Woburn Abbey is open between the 11th of April and the 28th of September from 11 am to 5 pm, with the last entry at 4 pm. The facility closes on 29th September until 24th October and then reopens on 25th October until 2nd November. The deer park, gardens, and grounds are open from the 11th of April until 2nd November from 10 am until 6 pm, with the last entry at 5 pm. They offer a variety of ticket options, whether you want to spend the day exploring the Abbey or a combined ticket to visit the Woburn Safari Park as well. You can also book a seat for afternoon tea in The Duchess' Tea Room. To view prices for different visitor packages and to read more about Woburn Abbey, visit the website at www.woburnabbey.co.uk.

LONGLEAT
Britain's First Safari Park

Key Facts about Longleat

- Longleat is a stately house situated in a 1,000-acre area of land near Warminster and Frome.
- It is the first safari park to be established outside of Africa.
- The house is currently the seat of the Marquess of Bath.
- Longleat has a variety of entertainment options, including a bat cave, penguin exhibit, and hedge maze.
- Visitors can rent various cottages around the property for a true safari experience.

The first stately home to open to the public as a tourist attraction was Longleat. It also has the first safari park to be established outside of Africa. If you are searching for a fun location where your family can enjoy outdoor entertainment with a mixture of history, then Longleat is a great spot to visit. The true beauty of the grounds is the immaculate house, which has a long-standing history.

The beautiful Longleat house is situated on a 1,000-acre area of land near the towns of Warminster, in Wiltshire, and Frome, in Somerset. The property was purchased by Sir John Thynn in 1540 for only £53. At that time, it was approximately 60 acres of land that contained the original house, an orchard, and a rabbit warren. The original house was burnt and destroyed during a fire in April 1567.

Sir John successfully rebuilt the house with the help of architects Adrian Gaunt, Robert Smythson, Alan Maynard, Humpfrey Lovell, and the Earl of Hertford. However, much of the design work was completed by Sir John. The house was fully completed by 1580. Sir John Thynn was the first of the Thynne dynasty. The spelling of the last name was changed to different variations throughout time. However, the current head of the family returned the name back to Thynn in the 1980s.

A variety of different nobles inherited the estate as the years progressed, each making different improvements or changes in the overall upkeep of the house. The 1st Viscount Weymouth, Thomas Thynne, created the large book collection in the house. He also commissioned the help of George London, Arnold Quellin, and Chevalier David to create the formal gardens, fountains, and canals.

Thomas also founded a boy's grammar school in 1707 in the town of Warminster. It later became known as the Lord Weymouth School, and in 1973, it merged with the St. Monica's School for Girls to create Warminster School. His son, also named Thomas, and the 2nd Viscount Weymouth, married Louisa Carteret. Her ghost is said to haunt the house.

The next heir, who began the Marquess nobility and carried on the name of Thomas, wanted to modernize the land to mirror that of other famous landscapes. He commissioned the famous Capability Brown to design a landscaped park that would replace the formal gardens, as well as add extra entrance roads and dramatic drives that viewers utilized when visiting. His son also worked to modernize the house by employing Jeffry Wyatville to demolish different parts of the house, which included a staircase, in order to build a larger staircase and a new gallery. He also built different buildings on the outside of the property, such as the Orangery.

The events of WWI brought a new need for the home when it was temporarily transformed into a hospital to help the soldiers. The house was also converted into a Royal School for Daughters of Officers of the Army during WWII. Unfortunately, the war had a negative impact on the overall finances of the estate. In order to pay for death duties, Henry Frederick Thynn had to sell a large portion of the estate's assets in 1947. He was also forced to open the house to the public in order for Longleat to prosper. The 7th Marquess of Bath, Alexander Thynn, was responsible for the creation of all of the maze designs on the property. He designed the creations himself. The house is still used as a private residence for the Thynn family.

What Makes This House Famous

The house is most famous for the safari and adventure parks that are present on the grounds. These features were first opened in 1966, and it is considered to be the first drive-through safari park outside of Africa. The safari park is considered to be a remarkable attraction, unique from other events located elsewhere. The animals are able to freely roam the grounds where they are contained, and the visitors are the ones who are in cages or, in reality, cars.

The safari park was an idea brainstormed by Jimmy Chipperfield, who is also the former co-director of Chipperfield's Circus. Today, there are 9,000 acres owned by the Longleat estate, in which 500 animals roam in a safe and humane environment. Other features include a bat cave, penguin exhibit, hedge maze, mirror maze, jungle railway, and other equally exciting entertainment.

For visitors who want a true safari experience, there are various cottages for rent around the property that put the visitor front and center of the safari action. They can wake up to see the sun rise over the African Village, which will make them feel as if they are literally in Africa. Other cottages include secluded locations around the property that provide a quiet and relaxing vacation.

While the Safari portion of the estate is highly sought after, the contents inside of the house are extremely popular. The house itself is packed with antiques and important artifacts from history. Along the ceilings of the house are ornate paintings that have made Longleat incredibly famous. The estate has introduced a new feature for guests: moving portraits. In the Great Hall, visitors can be in awe of two painted portraits that come to life. The paintings show the 2nd Viscount Weymouth, Thomas Thynne, and his wife Louisa arguing about the mysterious death of her manservant. There is also a ghostly vision of Louisa that floats throughout the house and visits many of the tours that are presented on the property.

The libraries in the house are also popular, with a total of over 40,000 books recorded in possession. Longleat is recorded as having one of the largest private book collections in Europe. In the Great Hall of Longleat, the waistcoat worn by King Charles I at his execution in 1649 is on display and still has the blood-stained silk sleeves intact. There are house tours that are performed every morning, lasting 40 minutes, that show many interesting antiques. Most of the contents within Longleat have been exempted from taxation. Due to this, some items are not able to be seen on a main visitor tour. Private tours are available that can show these rare items.

TV & Film Appearances

Longleat has been the host location for several film productions. The earliest was the 1959 film 'Libel,' in which Longleat is utilized as an estate location for Dirk Bogarde's character. It was also a location for the Bollywood film ' Mohabbatein,' as well as the location for the nature program 'Animal Park.' Other events include the estate being transformed into 'Memory Manor' for a memory skills program on the BBC and the location for the Red Bull Air Race in 2005.

Further Research

- Animal Park - BBC Series that chronicles the running of the safari park
- The history of Longleat by J. E. Jackson
- Longleat: The Story of an English Country House by David Burnett

Anglotopia's Take

Another one of our favorite places to visit in Britain. We've visited the house and Safari park several times over the years, and it's always worth a visit. We especially like to visit during the Christmas season, as they usually have a themed lights display that's quite a lot of fun. Longleat is the most 'touristy' place on the stately home trail - they even have a theme park on site. Still, despite this, there's still plenty of heritage to explore on-site, and the house itself is an incredible architectural wonder. With the recent death of the last

Marquess, there's no longer a lurid cloud hanging over the place as the new Marquess and his young family have taken over (and are no strangers to being on TV to promote the place).

Visiting Information

The Longleat House and Adventure Park are open daily except usually January through March when the house and safari park are closed. There are also periods throughout the year when they are open for a limited time, such as during the Christmas holiday or when there is inclement weather. They encourage everyone to verify with the website about opening availability if they are planning on visiting the safari excursion due to certain weather conditions that may limit the visibility of the animals. For more information about admission prices, opening and closing times, and other visiting information, check out the website: www.longleat.co.uk.

DYRHAM PARK
The House from Remains of the Day

Key Facts about Dyrham Park

- The original owner was Secretary of War to William III
- The name Dyrham is derived from the Saxon term 'Deor Hamm,' which means "deer enclosure."
- According to an Anglo-Saxon charter, the Saxons won a battle near Dyrham Park in 577 A.D.

Large and grand homes dot the English countryside. However, one mansion in particular is enriched in baroque design elements. Dyrham Park is nestled within a deer park, located near an ancient village in South Gloucestershire, England. The house itself is located within a parkland, which measures 274 acres. If you have a passion for historical landmarks, then continue reading for more information about Dyrham Park.

Dyrham Park is a baroque mansion that was purchased by William Blathwayt. He worked as a civil servant for many powerful names, such as Charles II, James II, and Queen Anne. He possessed a considerable amount of wealth due to the numerous fees he paid for the services that he provided, most of which were earned during his role as Surveyor and Auditor General of Plantation Revenues. Many governors of the colonies in Eastern America and in the Caribbean paid William to help expedite their business in London. Thanks to his success in this venture, he was able to purchase the materials needed to build Dyrham Park.

William Blathwayt married into money when he was wed to 36-year-old Mary Wynter, in 1686, the heiress to the Dyrham estate. After five years of marriage, Mary died, leaving William with three children: William, John, and Anne. The family that produced Mary purchased the original Dyrham Park in 1571. They were most commonly known as a naval family. Mary's grandfather, John Wynter, sailed with Sir Francis Drake in 1577. However, there were piracy accusations that almost brought the family into exile. Mary's mother and father had five children, with Mary being the only child who survived.

The house that is presently on the grounds today was built after Mary's death. However, William devoted a bedroom to his late wife's belongings to help with his grieving process. His daughter, Anne, married a man from a local family but died while she was delivering her first child during the first year of her marriage. William's second son, John, bought a commission in the Guards. It was William's oldest son, also named William, who later inherited the Dyrham Park estate.

The mansion was designed by two different architects. The West portion was commissioned in 1692 for the services of Samuel Hauduroy, and the East front was designed in 1704 by William Talman. Even though Blathwayt worked for many nobles, he was never given a noble status. In order to compensate for this, he built the mansion to show his wealth, as well as the elaborate gardens. He also filled the house with highly sought-after collectibles, decorations, and furniture. The original gardens contained elaborate cascades, fountains, statues, and a canal. However, by the late 1790s, it was somewhat unfashionable and difficult to maintain. A more simple and natural park was then constructed in its place.

Years later, William left his inheritance to his cousin, Colonel George Blathwayt, in 1844. Unfortunately, William's wife, Frances, gave all the contents of the Dyrham Park house to her family. George then raised £50,000 to buy the contents back from the family. He also spent an additional £23,000 on repairs for the house. This was a very large amount of money to spend in this time period – even today for most people.

The interior design and contents are still very much the

same as they were centuries ago. The house was inhabited by the Blathwayt family until 1956. In 1961, the property was acquired by the National Trust. However, the Blathwayt family motto is still present in the house. Above the west door of the mansion, you will see 'His Utere Mecum.' It translates to "share all of this with me."

What Makes This House Famous

Dyrham Park is mostly known because it was the filming location of the external scenes in The Remains of the Day. The exteriors stood in for Darlington Hall in the film. The interiors were filmed elsewhere. The landscape is also well known and it's a popular destination for families on days out.

TV & Film Appearances

Dyrham Park was featured in several film and TV productions. In 1993, it was used as a location for the film 'The Remains of the Day.' Also, an aerial view of the grounds was used in the opening section of the 2008 film 'Australia.' Lastly, the estate gardens were used in the outdoor scenes in the 1999 mini-series 'Wives and Daughters,' as well as in September 2010 for a scene in an episode of Doctor Who.

Anglotopia's Take

I'm a huge fan of the film The Remains of the Day, so I've visited this house a few times over the years. While the interiors were filmed elsewhere, it's worth visiting to see how the house is set in its landscape. It's so perfect it hurts! The house recently underwent significant conservation-restoration, so you will not see the house in a better state than it is now. But if you don't want to see the inside, visit on a day the house is closed, and go for a walk on the grounds. You have the place to yourself and can explore in peace and quiet. Be warned, though, while the walk to the house from the National Trust car park is a dawdle when you're going downhill to the house, it is quite a climb on the way back up!

Visiting Information

When arriving at Dyrham Park, you find that there is no car parking area close to the house. There's a lovely walk to the house, or there is a regular shuttle bus that delivers visitors from the car parking area to the house, shops, tea room, and gardens. There are no fees to park or to ride the bus (but there's no bus when the property is closed). The park welcomes families, large groups, and other specialized visitors every day of the year. Refer to the website for more information about admission and opening times: www.nationaltrust.org.uk/dyrham-park.

STOURHEAD
The Most Beautiful Gardens in England

Key Facts about Stourhead

- Stourhead was first built in the 18th century by the Hoare family, who were wealthy London bankers.
- Owned by the National Trust since 1946
- One of the first houses to be built in the Palladian style
- The gardens at Stourhead are some of the most beautiful in England and were designed by the famous landscape architect Capability Brown.
- Stourhead has been used as a filming location for a number of movies and TV shows, including Pride and Prejudice, Sense and Sensibility, and The Crown.

Stourhead House and Gardens is a true gem of England. Nestled in the Wiltshire countryside, the house and its surrounding gardens are a breathtaking sight to behold. The house, built in the 18th century, boasts a stunning collection of paintings, furniture, and decorative arts. But it is perhaps the gardens that are the true highlight of Stourhead. Designed to evoke the beauty of Ancient Greece and Rome, the gardens feature a picturesque lake, classical temples, and a plethora of exotic trees and plants, creating England's idea of Arcadia. It's no wonder that Stourhead has become a must-see attraction for visitors to England and one of the most popular gardens in the country. It also happens to be Anglotopia's favorite National Trust property and the one we have been to the most.

Prior to the acquisition by the Hoare family, the Stourhead estate was occupied by the Stourton family, known as the Barons of Stourton. They lived in the house for approximately 500 years and then sold the estate to Sir Thomas Meres in 1714. By this time,

Hoare's Bank had been established by Sir Richard Hoare, who had been knighted by Queen Anne for his accomplishments. Sir Richard came from humble beginnings as a horse dealer's son. His own son, Henry Hoare I, became a co-owner of the bank and utilized his wealth to purchase Stourton manor in 1717.

Henry chose to have the original house torn down and a new, modernized version built in its place. He renamed the house Stourhead, which is the name that we now know today. Architect Colen Campbell was hired to design the plans for Stourhead and utilized the help of Nathaniel Ireson to build the structure between 1721 and 1725 in the new Palladian style. It is one of England's first Palladian houses to be built.

The house is built of beautiful, honey-colored Bath stone and features a central block with two flanking wings, creating a symmetrical and balanced appearance. Stourhead House has impressive interiors, which are richly decorated with ornate plasterwork, elegant furnishings, and stunning artwork. The house has a grand entrance hall, a beautiful library, and an impressive staircase leading to the upper floors. The state rooms are particularly impressive, with their high ceilings, large windows, and intricate detailing.

Much of Stourhead's success can be accounted for by Henry Hoare II, who inherited the house after the death of his father, Henry Hoare I. He was an avid collector of paintings and sculptures, which he abundantly furnished the house with. He also created the legendary gardens that contain the temples and other monuments.

Henry Hoare II chose his grandson, Sir Richard Colt Hoare, as his heir to the estate. The only condition was that he was free to leave the banking business. Colt made extra alterations to the estate, which included adding two wings to each side of the house. Colt also hired the younger Thomas Chippendale to design and create furniture for all rooms in the house, which included a newly created library. He left the estate to his half-brother, Sir Henry Hugh Hoare, who later added the portico to the house. He was the owner of the property for only three years.

There were many inheritors of the Stourhead estate as the years progressed. One owner who had unfortunate luck with

finances was Sir Henry Ainslie Hoare. He was the nephew of one of the previous Hoare inhabitants. Sir Henry loved a flamboyant lifestyle, which later forced him to account for his debts and exiled him from the family. There was an heirloom sale in 1883 to help compensate for the loss of finances. Items sold at the sale included artwork by Poussin, Nicholson, and Turner. Sir Henry left the Stourhead estate in 1885.

The last family member to own the estate was Sir Henry Hugh Arthur Hoare. While in possession of the house, a fire occurred in 1902, which resulted in the loss of all of the furniture present on the top floors of the house. It also destroyed the central part of the house as well. Sir Henry made it his responsibility to restore the house to what it once was. The final renovations were completed in 1907.

He gave the property to the National Trust in 1946, which was ironically one year prior to his death. His only heir would have been his son, Captain Henry Colt Arthur Hoare, who served on the Queen's Own Dorset Yeomanry. However, he died in action at the Battle of Mughar Ridge on 13th November 1917 during WWI. There is a commemorative plaque located at Memorial Hall at Stourhead that honors Captain Henry Hoare for his duties.

What Makes This House Famous

The house is most commonly known for being the ancestral home of the Hoare's Bank founding family. It is currently the oldest privately owned bank in England, and it is still managed by Sir Richard Hoare's descendants. As mentioned earlier, the creation of the Stourhead Estate is closely related to the success of the Hoare family in the banking business. Other than being the son of a horse trader, Sir Richard Hoare established his humble beginnings with his goldsmith business in Cheapside, London. He then moved the business to 37 Fleet Street, where the Hoare's Bank is now located.

While poor investment choices and unwise management practices did cause some issues for the bank in the late 1800s, the business picked back up in the early 20th century. After WWI, many independent banks were being bought out by larger corporations. However, the Hoare family decided not to merge, which now gives them the title of the oldest independent bank in history.

While the house was given to the National Trust in 1946, a Hoare family descendent still has the right to live in the house in an apartment closed to the public.

The Gardens

While the house at Stourhead is recognized as a wonderful design in architectural history, the gardens are the most famous aspect of the estate, and most people don't even visit the house. Henry Hoare II created the design for the lake, temples, and other characteristics, which gave him the title "Henry The Magnificent." As a lover of Greek mythology, Henry designed the area to depict a journey that is similar to that of Aeneas's descent into the underworld. The overall layout is very similar to the 'genius of the place' concept that was made popular by Alexander Pope. There are numerous details located in the temples that surround the lake that tell of Aeneas's journey.

The temples and monuments are placed strategically around the lake to complement one another. For example, the Pantheon beckons the individual over, but once you are at the monument, you are given an exquisite view of the lake shore on the opposite side. A specially designed pathway also forces the eye from one monument to the other and allows the viewer to see all of the surrounding areas. The Pantheon is thought to be the most important structure on the grounds due to its presence in many of the artwork pieces that were owned by Henry.

The gardens were designed and completed between 1741 and 1780 through a carefully thought-out process by landscape designer Capability Brown. Henry had a small stream that was located on the grounds, widened, and created a large lake. The overall landscape of the gardens is very similar to the gardens at Stowe. Other structures present on the grounds include two Iron Age hill forts: Whitesheet and Park Hill Camp. On a hill overlooking the gardens is a 50-meter-tall tower known as King Alfred's Tower, which was designed by Henry Flitcroft in 1772.

Anglotopia's Take

This is the one British tourist attraction that we have visited the most in our over 20 years of travel in the UK. When we visit nearby Dorset, we always plan to visit here. It's the perfect National Trust experience. You can take a lovely stroll in the gardens, you can tour an amazing house, you can have a lovely meal in the cafe. It ticks all the boxes and during the deep, dark pandemic, it's the place I wanted to visit the most. There are plenty of finer and more famous stately homes to visit in Britain, and you should, but the scale of Stourhead is approachable. Most people, however, don't even visit the house because the gardens are what's most famous about Stourhead. Anyone who has seen the 2005 Pride & Prejudice has seen the gardens, and the Temple of Apollo is a must-visit for fans of the film. We have visited Stourhead in every season, and every time, even in the darkest of winter, it is English perfection.

TV & Film Appearances

The Stourhead Estate has been prominent in many TV and Film productions. Several works that are most famous for the use of the Stourhead location include:

- Temple of Apollo is featured in Pride & Prejudice (2005)
- A miniature replica of Stourhead was produced to be featured as the residence of Lady Penelope Creighton-Ward in the Thunderbirds TV series
- For the film 'Barry Lyndon,' the gardens were used as an appropriate film setting
- The Stourhead House was on the cover of the single 'What Will You Do (When The Money Goes)?' by Indie rock band Milburn.

Further Research

Available books:

- Stourhead - by Stephen Anderton and Alan Power
- Stourhead: Henry Hoare's Paradise Revisited by Dudley Dodd, Marianne Majerus, et al.

Visiting Information

Stourhead Estate is open every day of the year, except for a time period during winter when only the grounds are open to the public for various holiday events. Check the National Trust website or app for current opening times, as it can vary based on season and time. Select rooms of the house are decorated for Christmas every year during special openings in December. Refer to the Stourhead website for more information in order to plan your visit: www.nationaltrust.org.uk/stourhead.

HIGHCLERE CASTLE
AKA Downton Abbey

Key Facts about Highclere Castle

- An Anglo-Saxon charter proves that people have lived on the property for around 1300 years
- It is the current filming location for the popular TV series 'Downton Abbey'
- The 7th Earl of Carnarvon remained in great friendship with Queen Elizabeth II until his death in 2001.

This is probably the most famous English house in the world! If you possess a passion for grand English houses, then Highclere Castle should surely be on your list of favorites. Located just south of Newbury, Berkshire, in the county of Hampshire, is the settlement of Highclere Park, which hosts the location for this Jacobethan-style house. Measured at 5,000 acres, the estate is also the country seat for the Earl of Carnarvon. Highclere is most well known now as the fictional home of Downton Abbey, where the hit British TV show was filmed.

Highclere Castle is the second house to be built on the estate property. It was once a smaller estate that was built on the foundations of the medieval palace of the Bishops of Winchester, which dates back to the 8th century. The original site was actually recorded in the Domesday Book. However, it was in 1679 when the home was taken into the hands of the Carnarvon family.

During this time period, it was a square, classical-style

mansion. In 1692, the estate was gifted as a wedding present by Robert Sawyer to his daughter, Margaret, who married the 8th Earl of Pembroke. The second son of Margaret, Robert Sawyer Herbert, went on to inherit Highclere and made his own impact on the estate by creating the garden temple. His nephew and heir to the estate, Henry Herbert, later known as Baron Porchester, became the 1st Earl of Carnarvon by George III.

It was in 1838 that the 3rd Earl hired the help of Sir Charles Barry, the person responsible for the rebuilding of the Houses of Parliament. During this time period, there was a Renaissance Revival movement, which Barry was greatly skilled at creating. However, at Highclere, he designed the estate with Jacobethan style influences. There are touches of details that do reflect the Renaissance-based characteristics, such as the towers in the castle, which are slimmer than others built during the same time period. It is said that when Barry was creating a rough draft of the house design, he used all Italian Renaissance characteristics. However, it was rejected by the Earl.

The 3rd Earl died in 1849, and Sir Charles Barry died in 1860. At this time, the West Wing was still not completed. This was also where the servants' quarters were designated. The 4th Earl hired the services of architect Thomas Allom, who had worked with Barry in previous years, to help supervise the finished construction of the castle. It was completed in 1878.

During the 20th Century, Highclere Castle was the meeting place for all sorts of important people. Visitor books recorded that the house parties hosted at the castle were visited by Egyptologists, aviators, soldiers, technological innovators, and politicians. The 5th Countess of Carnarvon, Almina, transformed the house into a hospital during WWI to help soldiers coming home from Flanders in neighboring Belgium. Almina became a skilled nurse and healer, which was obvious from the numerous letters found from patients and their families who thanked her for her generosity.

In 1922, the castle was returned to a private home for the 5th Earl of Carnarvon and his family. After his death, his son returned to Highclere Castle, where he resided until 1986. The current resident is the 8th Earl and Countess of Carnarvon. By 2009, the Castle was in dire need of repairs. The only floors that were able to be used were the ground and first floors. Water damage had caused stonework to deteriorate and ceilings to crumble. More than 50 rooms were uninhabitable. This forced the 8th Earl and his family to live in a house nearby on the estate grounds.

The estimated cost for the repairs was around £12 million (around $20 million). Thanks to the increase in visitors since 2012 due to the success of Downton Abbey, the Earl and Lady Carnarvon have been able to perform major repairs on the Castle. The family lives in Highclere Castle during the winter months and then returns to their cottage during the summer when the castle is open to the public.

What Makes This House Famous

Highclere Castle is most famous for its appearance in the successful TV series Downton Abbey. Created by Julian Fellowes, the television drama was first aired in the United Kingdom on 26th September 2010 and in the United States on 9th January 2011. The series is set in a fictional estate called Downton Abbey (Highclere Castle), located in Yorkshire, and portrays the life of the Crawley family, including that of their servants. Contrary to where the show is set, the house is actually in the Home Counties of Southeast England in Hampshire (but its postcode address is in Berkshire as the closest town is Newbury in Berkshire — this leads to lots of confusion as to where the house actually is). The show is set in the post-Edwardian era and depicts how the great events of history have lasting effects on people in aristocratic positions. The show was not expected to last past the first season, but its fifth series is about to air in the UK.

TV & Film

Other TV and film appearances that utilized the Castle include The Secret Garden (1987), Eyes Wide Shut (1999), The Four Feathers (2002), and John Legend's music video for 'Heaven Only

Knows' (2006). Highclere Castle also rents its facilities for small film units and photography sessions, many of which are wedding events.

Further History

The 5th Earl of Carnarvon discovered a Tomb that contained the Egyptian Boy Pharaoh, Tutankhamun, during an archaeological dig in 1922 with the help of his colleague, Howard Carter. They both spent 16 years working together through various excavation trips in Egypt. The Earl also helped Carter build a house in the desert close to the Valley of the Kings, which was properly nicknamed 'Castle Carter.' Both men were convinced that there were more tombs located in the Valley of the Kings. To help prove their hypothesis, they created a grid system in order to document where they had already excavated.

In the autumn of 1922, they planned one last excursion, in which the Earl's daughter, Lady Evelyn, also accompanied the men. Their trip was obviously a success due to the discovery of the Egyptian Boy Pharaoh. After the death of the 5th Earl, his widow sold his collection to the Metropolitan Museum in New York in order to pay for death duties. However, not all artifacts had been sold; instead, they were tucked away in cupboards until they were rediscovered by the Carnarvon family in 1987.

To help celebrate the success of the 5th Earl's accomplishment, the current Earl and Countess have opened an Egyptian Exhibition in the cellars of the Castle. This is also referred to as the 'Discovery Gallery,' which highlights different events that occurred for the Carnarvon family during the Great War, unfortunate financial situations, and the overall discovery of Egyptian artifacts.

Anglotopia's Take

If you're a fan of Downton Abbey, then visiting this house is a must! It's hard to get to, and it's only open on certain days of the year. You must book and plan ahead, but I recommend going on a scheduled tour excursion that visits the house when it's not normally open. Otherwise, the house is very, very crowded on open days (and securing tickets can be a challenge as they limit spots, and it sells out). You can easily spend all day here. If you're looking for Downton Abbey merchandise in the gift shop, you will be disappointed. Don't expect to find Downton Village nearby, as that was filmed elsewhere (Bampton in Oxfordshire).

Further Research

- Secrets of Highclere Castle - PBS Documentary
- Christmas at Highclere: Recipes and Traditions from The Real Downton Abbey by The Countess of Carnarvon
- Lady Almina and the Real Downton Abbey: The Lost Legacy of Highclere Castle by Countess of Carnarvon
- At Home at Highclere: Entertaining at the Real Downton Abbey by The Countess of Carnarvon

Visiting Information

Highclere Castle is open on approximately 70 days each year. They are open for a period of two weeks during the Easter holiday and May Bank holidays and for a duration of two months during the summer, Sunday through to Thursday. They also open for a few days in December to celebrate the Christmas holidays. There are guides in the rooms of the castle and in the cellar discovery area to provide unknown or behind-the-scenes information that is not typically broadcast. They offer various discounted rates for large groups and school visits. Refer to their website for complete information about planning your visit: www.highclerecastle.co.uk. Tickets must be booked in advance and often sell out months ahead of time, so planning ahead is critical.

CASTLE HOWARD
The Real Brideshead

Key Facts about Castle Howard

- Construction took over 100 years to complete
- The estate was once served by its own railway station
- Most famous as the setting of the fiction house Brideshead inBrideshead Revisited (both the TV Series and Film)
- The castle was awarded the 2014 Certificate of Excellence by Trip Advisor.

Castle Howard, located in North Yorkshire, is one of the most treasured homes in England. It has been the home to the Howard family for over 300 years and is still a private residence for the current Howard family. While the house is not a real castle, it was given the name as a standard for all houses that are built on the site of a former military castle. The house is most famous as the filming location for the 1980s miniseries Brideshead Revisited (and was so iconic that it was used again for the 2005 film remake.

The original site where Castle Howard was built was originally the location of another ruined castle known as Henderskelfe Castle. It was inherited by the Howard family in 1566. Construction of the castle was originally started in 1699; however, it took a lifespan of three different Howard Earls and various architects to complete. The 3rd Earl of Carlisle commissioned the services of Vanbrugh, a member of the Kit-Cat Club, to design the plans for Castle Howard. It was actually his first architectural project. Vanbrugh was assisted by Nicholas Hawksmoor. His designs reflected a Baroque style, with two wings on each side of the structure. The dome was not part of the original plans and was added after the building had already begun.

Construction was started at the east end, with the East Wing being completed between 1701 and 1703. Other finished areas included the east end of the garden entrance, the Central Block, which included the dome, and the west end of the garden front entrance. The finishing touches included an exuberant amount of baroque qualities, such as cherubs, urns, coronets, and Roman Doric pilasters. Much of the dome interior was painted by Giovanni Antonio Pellegrini.

Although the West Wing was not completed, the Earl decided to focus on the exterior portion, such as the gardens and surrounding grounds. At this stage, it had cost the 3rd Earl of Carlisle almost 30% of his entire income. The 4th Earl was responsible for the completion of the West Wing. However, the first floor and the roof were not complete when the death of the 4th Earl occurred. The rooms of Castle Howard were completed in different stages over the years, and the overall completion did not occur until 1811. During the time of the 7th Earl of Carlisle, the estate covered 13,000 acres and included the villages of Coneysthrope, Terrington, Bulmer, Slingsby, and Welburn. The estate was also serviced by its own railway station from 1845 to the mid-1950s.

Unfortunately, a large portion of the house was destroyed during a fire on 9th November 1940. The fire started as a chimney fire in the southeast corner of the south wing and spread throughout the building. The central hall, dome, dining room, and staterooms on the east side of the house were destroyed. This included paintings that depicted the Fall of Phaeton by Antonio Pellegrini. A total of 20 paintings were ruined. It took a number of county fire brigades a total of 8 hours to finally diminish.

During the 1960s, the dome was rebuilt, as well as a recreation of Pellegrini's paintings. The Howards have continuously taken up residency at Castle Howard ever since it was built by the 3rd Earl of Carlisle. There was one brief period during World War II when it was utilized as a girls' school. The house was officially opened to the public in 1952 by George Howard. It is now owned by his son, Simon Howard, who lives at the house with his wife, son, and daughter.

What Makes This House Famous

The house is a stunning surviving example of English Baroque architecture, and the home became iconic due to its role in the TV series and later film adaptation of Brideshead Revisited. Other than the incredible rehabilitation after the house fire, another factor that has made Castle Howard so famous today is the surrounding villages that the estate owns. There are approximately 170 residential properties available to rent that are owned by the Castle Howard Estate. They range from large family houses to cottages and flats. Many of the staff members who work at Castle Howard live in these properties. There are also 14 commercial properties, which include offices, workshops, livery businesses, shops, and garages. The estate is also relied upon for two village schools, attached playing fields, garden allotments, village halls, and mooring rights on the River Derwent.

One interesting feature of Castle Howard is the Chapel. It was built during the 18th-century construction of the West Wing. An interesting fact to note is that it was originally meant to be a dining room. In 1870, it was dramatically reconstructed, with the entrance completely changed and the floor lowered to create higher ceilings. It was also redesigned in a pre-Raphaelite style with exceptional designs created by William Morris and Edward Burne-Jones. Modern touches have been added to allow for more lighting, including the addition of a state-of-the-art LED lighting system.

The features of Castle Howard are not solely contained within the house. Other beautiful sights to be seen include the gardens and other exterior landscapes. The house itself is situated on a ridge, which then opens up to a large park that contains a lake on each side of the house, two garden structures which include the Temple of the Four Winds and the Mausoleum, an arboretum, a walled garden, and other eye-catching garden features.

TV & Film Appearances

Castle Howard has been the center stage for many films and TV productions. Sophia Loren starred in 'Lady L' in 1965, which was filmed at the castle. Ten years later, 'Barry Lyndon,' directed by Stanley Kubrick, was filmed on the castle grounds. Other popular productions include the TV production of Brideshead in 1981, Brideshead Revisited in 2008, The Buccaneers in 1995, and Garfield: A Tail of Two Kitties, which was released in 2006. Most recently, the popular rendition of 'Death Comes to Pemberley' was filmed inside Castle Howard in 2013 (the exteriors were filmed at Chatsworth).

Further Research

- Castle Howard: The Biography by Christopher Ridgway
- Castle Howard: An Architectural History by Nicholas Savage
- Castle Howard: The Treasure House of England by Gervase Jackson-Stops
- Castle Howard: A Visitor's Guide by Simon Jenkins
- The Gardens of Castle Howard by Robin Whalley
- Castle Howard: A Noble Residence by Mark Bence-Jones
- The Howard Papers: The Letters and Papers of Sir Henry Howard, Third Earl of Surrey by Alan Stewart and Heather Wolfe
- The History of Castle Howard by Thomas Dunham Whitaker
- Castle Howard and Its Owners: A Family Portrait by the Earl of Carlisle
- Castle Howard: The Official Guide by Christopher Ridgway.

Visiting Information

The house is open to the public every day of the year except Christmas. You can tour the house on your own, or you can go on a private, curator-led tour that is a popular activity at the castle, in which visitors can learn more unknown facts about the property. There are different tours for each area of the property, and they are all booked by appointment only. Families are widely accepted and encouraged to visit Castle Howard. There are various festivals and family activities held at the estate each year. For more information and details on the private tours, family activities, opening and closing times, and the cost for admission, visit the Castle Howard website: www.castlehoward.co.uk.

Getting there: A car is the easiest way to get to Castle Howard; it is just 15 miles northeast of York and easily accessible from the A64, which connects Leeds, York, and the Yorkshire Coast. You can take a train to York and then take a local bus to the house, or you can hire a taxi. Public transport information here.

HARDWICK HALL
Bess of Hardwick's Palace

Key Facts about Hardwick Hall

- Built between 1590 and 1597 for the formidable Bess of Hardwick
- Currently owned by the National Trust
- Most of the furniture and other contents of the house date back to as early as 1601
- There are six rooftop sculptures on the outside that have the initials 'ES,' which stands for 'Elizabeth Shrewsbury.'

Hardwick Hall is a magnificent and historically significant estate located in Derbyshire, England. It was built between 1590 and 1597 for Elizabeth Shrewsbury, better known as Bess of Hardwick, one of the most influential women of her time. The house was designed by renowned architect Robert Smythson, and it is considered to be one of the finest examples of Elizabethan architecture in the country. Hardwick Hall has a fascinating history and has been home to many notable figures over the centuries, including King Charles I and his queen, Henrietta Maria. Today, the house and its beautiful gardens are open to the public, offering a unique glimpse into the past and a chance to marvel at the architectural and historical significance of this remarkable estate.

Bess of Hardwick came from a humble origin, but she later became one of the most powerful people next to Queen Elizabeth I. She was married four times, gaining more power after each marriage. After she married Sir William Cavendish, she convinced him to move back to her home county. As a native of Derbyshire,

Bess was very fond of the scenery and the quiet environment. They purchased the property for their well-known home, Chatsworth House, in 1549 and began building in 1552.

Bess married two more men over the course of 10 years, her last being the Earl of Shrewsbury, who was one of the richest and most powerful English nobles. The Shrewsburys were guardians of Mary, Queen of Scots, for many years while she was held captive at Chatsworth House. Bess is also the direct ancestress of the Dukes of Devonshire.

The story told is that Bess had a terrible argument with her husband, the Earl of Shrewsbury, and left their home at Chatsworth in 1584. She then organized plans to rebuild the Old Hall at Hardwick to create a new home for herself. However, her plans changed in 1590 when the Earl died, which left her with his inheritance. Due to her new positive financial situation, Bess decided to build a new construction at Hardwick, eliminating the renovation plans for the Old Hall altogether and creating the New Hall. She moved into her new house in October 1597.

Her new Hardwick Hall was a true statement of her power and wealth. It contained numerous windows that were exceptionally large for the time period. Glass was a luxury, and the house was described as being more glass than walls. The chimneys were also built into the internal walls instead of being constructed on the outside. This was done to allow more room for the large windows without weakening the exterior structure. An added touch by Bess was the carved 'ES' initials that are present in 6 of the rooftop sculptures at the head of each tower.

Hardwick is one of the first houses in England where the hall was built on an axis directly through the center of the house instead of at right angles to the entrance. The height of each ceiling is also unique, with each floor being slightly higher than the first. There are three main levels of the Hall, with the bottom level being smaller in height than the top floor. This was designed for the occupants of each room: the least important occupants stayed on the bottom floor, and the most important lived at the top. This helped to clearly designate the servants from the noble occupants.

The true treasure of Hardwick Hall is the remarkable

contents inside that were collected by the Countess. An exceptionally unique collection of paintings and furniture from the 16th century is still present inside. The Hall is fully furnished, exactly as Bess would have kept it. The second floor of the house contains the largest long gallery that has ever been present in an English house. The most notable features are the tapestries and needlework on display. Much of the needlework art has the 'ES' initials, and it is therefore assumed that Bess herself created much of it.

After the death of Bess in 1608, her son William Cavendish, the 1st Earl of Devonshire, inherited Hardwick Hall. His great-grandson, also named William, was titled as the 1st Duke of Devonshire, which began the Dukes of Devonshire dynasty. Chatsworth was and is the primary seat for the Dukes of Devonshire. However, Hardwick Hall remained a secondary home for the family to escape from the attention of the public. The family donated the house to the British government in 1956 in lieu of Death Duties, who then transferred the house to the National Trust. The house still stands and is surrounded by a walled garden, which includes an orchard, an herb garden, a café, and a National Trust gift shop.

What Makes This House Famous

Other than the exceptionally unique use of windows throughout the house, another fact that makes Hardwick Hall famous is that the 'Old Hall' is listed as an official ruin. It is present beside the New Hardwick Hall and was Bess's original home before she built the new house. The property is owned by the National Trust and administrated by English Heritage.

TV & Film Appearances

Hardwick Hall is most popular in the TV and film industry as the location for the exterior scenes of Malfoy Manor in Harry Potter and the Deathly Hallows – Part 1 and Part 2. The property was also used in the Connections TV series, which illustrated changes in home design, as well as the TV series Mastercrafts.

Anglotopia's Take

When exploring the English Midlands, Hardwick Hall is a great place to stop and explore. Bess of Hardwick was a fascinating and formidable woman, and it's quite something to explore her palace. It is a palace in everything but name. It has stunning architecture, a fascinating history, and a great National Trust property. Also, don't forget to visit the ruined 'old' Hardwick Hall.

Further Research on Hardwick Hall

- Venus in Winter: A Novel of Bess of Hardwick is a novel by Gillian Bagwell and is a fictionalization of Bess's life.
- Bess of Hardwick: Empire Builder by Mary S. Lovell

Visiting Information

Hardwick Hall, as well as the gardens, the shop, and the restaurant, are open most days of the week with the exception of bank holidays. They also have a period of time after Christmas when the house is closed. According to their website, the house opens back up to the public on 16th February. Before planning your visit, it is best to refer to their website in order to verify that they are open, as well as hours of operation and ticket prices. You can find the information at www.nationaltrust.org.uk/hardwick.

BLENHEIM PALACE
Churchill's Birthplace and Spiritual Home

Key Facts about Blenheim Palace

- Originally built as a gift to John Churchill, the 1st Duke of Marlborough
- Construction started in 1705 and lasted until 1722
- A designated UNESCO World Heritage Site in 1987
- The birthplace of Sir Winston Churchill
- Still owned by the ancestral Churchill family

The only non-royal country house in England to be titled as a palace is Blenheim Palace. This large estate is located in Woodstock, Oxfordshire, England. It is the current residence of the Duke and Duchess of Marlborough and was the birthplace of Sir Winston Churchill. As one of the largest houses in England, this is one location that is a must-see on your visitor itinerary.

Blenheim Palace was constructed between 1705 and 1722 as a gift to the 1st Duke of Marlborough. As the military commander, he led the allied forces to success in the Battle of Blenheim on 13th August 1704. The Duke won the battle when he received the surrender of Marshall Tallard, the leader of the French forces.

In return for his success, Queen Anne granted the Churchill family access to the Royal Manor and the park at Woodstock, as well as any funds necessary to build the Blenheim Palace. As a thank you for the gift, the Duke promised to address the Palace as a monument to Queen Anne.

The construction of the Palace took longer than normal due to several problems: the first being that Sarah, the 1st Duchess of Marlborough, did not have a desire for such a large house. She had preferred a smaller country house that was more suitable for comfort. She was also a very outspoken woman and did not hesitate to voice her unhappiness with the architect. This also caused her to fall out of favor with Queen Anne.

The architect selected for the ambitious project was controversial. The Duchess was known to favor Sir Christopher Wren, who was famous for St Paul's Cathedral and many other national buildings. The Duke, however, following a chance meeting at a playhouse, is said to have commissioned Sir John Vanbrugh there and then. Vanbrugh, a popular dramatist, was an untrained architect who usually worked in conjunction with the trained and practical Nicholas Hawksmoor. The duo had recently completed the first stages of the Baroque Castle Howard. This huge Yorkshire mansion was one of England's first houses in the flamboyant European Baroque style. Marlborough had obviously been impressed by this grandiose pile and wished for something similar at Woodstock.

A second problem arose when the funds being utilized to construct the house ran dry. Sarah was friends with Queen Anne prior to her receiving the title of Queen. She had a great influence over Queen Anne, both personally and politically. However, as years passed, the two grew apart, and it was finally the quarrel about the house that caused the two to part ways.

The building process was paused in the summer of 1712 when the funds for the construction were terminated by the Queen. This forced the Duke to complete the construction out of his own personal funds. A short time after, the Marlboroughs decided to go into exile and later returned after the death of the Queen on 1st August 1714.

Blenheim, however, was not to provide Vanbrugh with the architectural plaudits he imagined it would. The fight over funding led to accusations of extravagance and impracticability of design, many of these charges leveled by the Whig factions in power. He found no defender in the Duchess of Marlborough. Having been foiled in her wish to employ Wren, she leveled criticism at Vanbrugh on every level, from design to taste. In part, their problems arose from what was demanded of the architect. The nation (who it was then assumed, by architect and owners, was paying the bills) wanted a monument, but the Duchess wanted not only a fitting tribute to her husband but also a comfortable home, two requirements that were not compatible in 18th-century architecture. Finally, in the early days of the building, the Duke was frequently away on his military campaigns, and it was left to the Duchess to negotiate with Vanbrugh. More aware than her husband of the precarious state of the financial aid they were receiving, she attempted to curb Vanbrugh's grandiose ideas in an arrogant fashion (as was her wont) rather than explain the true reasons behind her frugality.

Following their final altercation, Vanbrugh was banned from the site. In 1719, while the Duchess was away, Vanbrugh viewed the palace in secret. However, when he and his wife, with the Earl of Carlisle, visited the completed Blenheim as members of the viewing public in 1725, they were refused admission even to enter the park. The palace had been completed by Nicholas Hawksmoor, his friend and architectural associate.

Blenheim Palace was the home to the Churchill family for 300 years. However, it was not free from ruin. At the end of the 19th century, the 9th Duke of Marlborough married the heiress to the American railroad, Consuelo Vanderbilt. With the newly found financial relief, the Palace was saved from the ruins, and a new restoration process began to bring it back to what it once was.

Many of the Duke's that have taken residence at the Palace have been especially involved in the improvements made to the property. The park and gardens underwent major changes when the 4th Duke commissioned the services of landscape designer Lancelot Brown and architect designer William Chambers.

Another Duke to make positive changes to the Palace was the 8th Duke. He was responsible for the introduction of electricity, gas, central heating, and an internal telephone system to be implemented in the house. Other restorations completed included the restoration of the State Rooms and added furniture throughout the Palace. This was completed by the 9th Duke.

The current Duke, who is also the 12th to carry the title, has made it his commitment to preserve the previous restorations completed, and it was also thanks to his father (the 11th Duke) that the property became a World Heritage Site in 1987.

What Makes This House So Famous

There are many stories about Blenheim that have made the property well known. However, the most famous reason is Sir Winston Churchill. He was born at the Blenheim Palace on 30th November 1874. He was the grandson of the 7th Duke, and he was also a close friend to the 9th Duke and Duchess. It was also at the small lake-side summerhouse near the Palace, known as "The Temple of Diana," where Winston Churchill proposed to his future wife, Miss Clementine Hozier, in 1908.

Their marriage was not expected to last, according to many critics, but the couple proved everyone wrong when their marriage lasted for 56 years. When Sir Winston Churchill died on 24th January 1965, he was an accomplished former British Prime Minister, author, painter, and historian. He was buried next to his parents in the cemetery of St. Martin's Church in Bladon, not far from the Blenheim Palace. Lady Churchill died 12 years later, and her cremated remains were laid to rest next to her husband.

TV & Film

The Palace has been the location for many popular films and television productions. With the excellent architecture and the breathtaking scenery, it is no surprise that the setting has been sought after by so many directors. The Blenheim Palace is not always center stage in a film. In some cases, it is part of a small scene, such as a skit on a staircase or in one of the gardens. Famous films that have been filmed at the Palace include: Young Winston (1972); Indiana Jones and the Last Crusade (1989); Black Beauty (1994); Harry Potter and the Order of the Phoenix (2007); The Young Victoria (2008); and Gulliver's Travels (2010).

Anglotopia's Take

If you're a Churchillian, then along with Chartwell, this is the one other place you should be sure to visit. You will learn about the long history of the Churchill family and how Winston came from warrior stock. While Chartwell was where Churchill lived, Blenheim was his spiritual home and the source of his energy and inspiration. So much so that he's buried nearby in the Bladon churchyard, his birth room has been preserved (along with the addition of some of his paintings), and the house definitely takes advantage of its connections. Truly one of the treasure houses of England.

Further Research

There are several books worth reading about the palace, including Blenheim: Biography of a Palace by Martin Fowler and Blenheim And the Churchill Family: A Personal Portrait, which was actually written by a member of the Marlborough family. The Palace was also featured in Treasure Houses of Britain, which is available on DVD and On Demand.

Visiting Information

The Palace is open to the public daily from 15th February to 2nd November, and Wednesdays through to Sundays from 5th November to 14th December. Each section of the property has a separate opening and closing time. Refer to the Blenheim Palace website for more information about specific opening and closing times, ticket prices, and direction information. You can easily spend the whole day on the estate, and there is plenty to do for the whole family.

CHATSWORTH
The Seat of the Cavendish Family

Key Facts about Chatsworth House

- It is the current seat for the Duke of Devonshire.
- Approximately located 5.6 km northeast of Bakewell and 14 miles west of Chesterfield.
- The house, which is backed by wooded hills, faces the land that divides the Wye and Derwent valleys.
- Long standing structure of history, including the home to Mary, Queen of Scots.
- Pemberley in the 2005 film version of Pride and Prejudice

Chatsworth House is a grand and magnificent estate located in the heart of England, in the county of Derbyshire. With over 400 years of history, the house has been home to some of the most famous and influential families in British history, including the Cavendish family. Known for its exceptional beauty, remarkable architecture, and stunning gardens, Chatsworth House has been a popular tourist destination for centuries. The house is an embodiment of the rich cultural heritage of England and an important part of British history. It is a must-see attraction for anyone interested in history, architecture, and the arts.

The origin of Chatsworth House dates back to the Elizabethan era and begins with a woman named Elizabeth Talbot, Countess of Shrewsbury. She is well known as Bess of Hardwick. As a native of Derbyshire, Bess was raised by a modest family. But she later became one of the second most powerful women, next to Queen Elizabeth I. She was married a total of four times, and it was after her marriage to her second husband, Sir William Cavendish, that the Cavendish history at Chatsworth House became what it is today.

Sir William Cavendish originated in Suffolk and became a powerful ally of King Henry VIII during the 16th century when he helped dissolve the monasteries. It was after his marriage to Bess that he agreed to move to her home county despite the remote location and the obvious flooding issues. They purchased the Chatsworth land in 1549 for a mere £600. However, it was not until 1552 that they began to build the first house.

After the death of Sir William Cavendish in 1557, Bess married two more men over the course of 10 years. Her last husband, George Talbot, the 6th Earl of Shrewsbury, was the primary appointed custodian of Mary, Queen of Scots. From 1569 to 1584, Mary was held as a prisoner at Chatsworth countless times. Her lodgings were not too shabby, though. She had her own rooms on the east side of the estate, which are still referred to as the Queen of Scots Apartments.

Bess is also known for Hardwick Hall, which is a surviving house that contains tapestries, furniture, and embroideries from the 16th and 17th centuries. It was in the possession of the Cavendish Family until 1957, when it was donated to the government to pay for death duties. It is now a National Trust property (we have an article about this house coming up in a few weeks).

During her marriage to Sir William Cavendish, Bess produced two sons, one of whom became the first Earl of Devonshire. He was also named Sir William Cavendish and later became the heir to the Cavendish fortune. When Bess died in 1608, the Earl inherited four valuable houses, which included Hardwick Hall, Chatsworth House, Oldcotes, and Worksop in Nottinghamshire. The Cavendish name was carried on with William's marriage to Anne Keighley, who produced three sons and three daughters.

The Cavendish name continued on for centuries, with many heirs carrying on the name of Sir William Cavendish. The 6th Duke of Devonshire, William Spencer Cavendish, is still remembered as the "Bachelor" Duke. He was never married but possessed a charming personality with many years spent entertaining friends and improving his inherited houses. William was responsible for the completion of the North Wing at Chatsworth, which was designed by architect Sir Jeffry Wyatville.

He also hired the specialties of a young gardener named Joseph Paxton to help evolve the gardens at Chatsworth into the beautiful masterpiece that exists today. William Spencer Cavendish died in 1858 at the age of 67. Since he had no direct descendants, the title of Duke was passed to his cousin, William Cavendish, the 2nd Earl of Burlington.

Most of the UK's country houses were put to institutional use during World War II. Some of those used as barracks were badly damaged, but the 10th Duke, anticipating that schoolgirls would make better tenants than soldiers, arranged for Chatsworth to be occupied by Penrhos College, a girls' public school in Colwyn Bay, Wales. The contents of the house were packed away in eleven days, and in September 1939, 300 girls and their teachers moved in for a six-year stay. The whole of the house was used, including the staterooms, which were turned into dormitories. Condensation from the breath of the sleeping girls caused fungus to grow behind some of the pictures. The house was not very comfortable for so many people, with a shortage of hot water, but there were compensations, such as skating on the Canal Pond. The girls grew vegetables in the garden as a contribution to the war effort.

The modern history of Chatsworth begins in 1950. The family had not yet moved back after the war, and although the 10th Duke had transferred his assets to his son during his lifetime in the hope of avoiding death duties, he died a few weeks too early for the lifetime exemption to apply, and tax was charged at 80% on the whole estate. The amount due was £7 million (£203 million as of 2014). Some of the family's advisors considered the situation to be irretrievable, and there was a proposal to transfer Chatsworth to the nation as a V&A of the North; instead, the Duke decided to retain his family's home if he could. He sold tens of thousands of acres of land, transferred Hardwick Hall to the National Trust in lieu of tax, and sold some major works of art from Chatsworth.

The 10th Duke was pessimistic about the future of houses like Chatsworth and made no plans to move back in after the war. After Penrhos College left in 1945, the only people who slept in the house were two housemaids, but over the winter of 1948–49, the house was cleaned and tidied to reopen it to the public. In

the mid-1950s, the 11th Duke and Duchess began to think about moving into the house. The pre-war house had relied entirely on a large staff for its comforts and lacked modern facilities. The building was rewired, the plumbing and heating were overhauled, and six self-contained staff flats were created to replace the small staff bedrooms and communal servants' hall. Including those in the staff flats, seventeen bathrooms were added to the existing handful. The 6th Duke's cavernous kitchen was abandoned, and a new one was created closer to the family dining room. The family rooms were repainted, carpets were brought out of the store, and curtains were repaired or replaced. The Duke and Duchess and their three children moved across the park from Edensor House in 1959.

In 1981, the family trustees created a separate charitable trust called 'The Chatsworth House Trust' to preserve the house and its setting. This trust was granted a 99-year lease by the Trustees of the Chatsworth Settlement of the house, its essential contents, the garden, the park, and some woods, a total of 1,822 acres (7.37 km2). The Chatsworth House Trust pays an annual rent of £1. The family sold some works of art, mainly old master drawings that could not be put on regular display, to raise a multimillion-pound endowment fund. The family is represented on the trust council, but the majority is made up of non-family members. The family pays a market rent for the use of its private apartments in the house. The cost of running the house and grounds is around £4 million a year.

The current occupant of Chatsworth House is Peregrine Cavendish, the 12th Duke of Devonshire, and his wife Amanda, the Duchess of Cavendish. They have three children: William, the Earl of Burlington, Lady Celina, and Lady Jasmine. The Duke and Duchess have ten grandchildren. There are many works of art displayed around the gardens and in the house for visitors to appreciate. This is a shared passion between the Duke and Duchess and their son, Lord Burlington.

A master plan to begin improvements on the house was formulated in 2008. This was organized after countless research studies and analyses proved specific services that could be utilized to help bring the Chatsworth House up to modern standards. This includes improvements made to the route that visitors utilize and extensive preservation of the exterior stone.

Chatsworth has been selected as the United Kingdom's favorite country house several times and continues to be one of its most popular tourist attractions.

What Makes This House So Famous

Many popular names have come through the Chatsworth House. In 1944, the sister of John F. Kennedy, Kathleen Kennedy, was married to William Cavendish, the eldest son of the 10th Duke of Devonshire. However, this was a tragic and short-lived marriage due to the fact that William was killed in action not long after their marriage. Kathleen died in 1948 in a plane crash. William's younger brother, Andrew Cavendish, took the title of 11th Duke and later married Deborah Mitford.

TV & Film

The Chatsworth House has been the location for numerous film and TV locations. The first was the 1975 adaptation of the novel 'The Luck of Barry Lyndon' by William Thackeray. It was also the location for the 2005 version of Pride and Prejudice, and the 2013 television version of Death Comes to Pemberley by P.D. James, which is a sequel to Pride and Prejudice. The actual house is mentioned in the P.D. James novel as one of the locations that Elizabeth Bennett visits before her arrival at Pemberley. Other films that utilized the Chatsworth House for location were The Duchess in 2008 and The Wolfman in 2010. It is believed that Jane Austen chose the Chatsworth House when she was writing Pride and Prejudice based on her description of Pemberley.

Anglotopia's Take

Another treasure house of England that epitomizes what people imagine of England when they think of a stately home in the countryside. This grand house, which recently completed a multiyear restoration and conservation program (and no longer has scaffolding on it for the first time in decades), is situated perfectly in its Arcadian landscape. It is one of the few houses still in the hands of the original family, who also still live in it and manage its day-to-day operations (which have been the subject of several television shows). Used often as a filming location for period dramas, Chatsworth is a must-visit for any stately home enthusiast.

Further Research

- Chatsworth - 2012 - Documentary series on Amazon Prime Video
- Chatsworth: Its gardens and the people who made them by Alan Titchmarsh
- Chatsworth, Arcadia Now: Seven Scenes from the Life of an English Country House - by John-Paul Stonard (Author), Victoria Hely-Hutchinson (Photographer)
- Secrets of Chatsworth - PBS Documentary
- Georgiana: Duchess of Devonshire – by Amanda Foreman

Visiting Information

Chatsworth House is open every day from March through December. The opening times for all of the different features of Chatsworth House vary depending on the category, such as restaurants and shopping ventures. Before planning your visit, it is best to check out the official website, www.chatsworth.org. There are also options for purchasing visitor tickets via their website.

WOKEFIELD PARK
An 18th Century Masterpeice

Key Facts about Wokefield Park

- Wokefield Park is located in the parish of Wokefield, near Mortimer in Berkshire.
- Built around the mid-18th century, there has been a manor recorded on the site of Wokefield Park since 1086.
- Wokefield Park is now a conference center and events venue with an 18-hole golf course managed by the De Vere group.

Wokefield Park is a fairly typical 18th-century country house. No one can say precisely when the house was built or who it was built for, but a manor at Wokefield is mentioned in the Domesday Book of 1086. The deeds for Wokefield Park have passed through the hands of many owners and many families over the years before ending up in the hands of the De Vere Hotel Company, who have transformed the mansion house into a conference center and popular wedding venue.

Most accounts of the history of Wokefield Park only stretch back to around the year 1777, when the Brocas family acquired the property and began making alterations. However, evidence of a manor at Wokefield goes back much farther than that, as far as 1086, in fact, as Wokefield is first mentioned on paper in William the Conqueror's Domesday Book. Wokefield Manor was assessed at one and ½ hides and was said to belong to Walter, the son of Other. Walter's descendants, the Danver family, held the over-lordship of Wokefield Manor until the year 1321, when Sir Thomas Danvers granted the manor to Roger Mortimer.

Just 19 years later, in 1340, the king granted Wokefield Manor to John Brocas, and the lands became the property of the Brocas family for the next 100 years. Wokefield Manor was restored back to the Mortimer family next and followed the descent of Stratfield Mortimer until 1553. It was at this time that the current house standing at Wokefield Park may have come into existence. Around 1569, Wokefield Manor was sold to Edmund Plowden, treasurer of the Middle Temple. The current house features a vaulted cellar that is thought to date back to this time. A loyal Roman Catholic, considered the best scholar of the law in the country, Plowden lived at Wokefield Park until his death in 1585.

The majority of Wokefield Park, as it stands today, is believed to have been built for owner Bernard Brocas of Beaurepaire at some time in the mid-18th century. A large symmetrical building with a central block of three stories, Wokefield Park is typical of 18th-century country houses. On the north front is a portico of Doric Stone, and the house features a decorative Roman cement facing with a slate roof. The interiors at Wokefield Park are notable for their 18th century stairway with a molded handrail and twisted balusters.

Alterations have been made to Wokefield Park continually since the 18th century, with subsequent owners, such as George Palmer MP, making their own mark on the property. Much of the interior is now a restoration of 19th-century designs featuring contemporary fireplaces, wood paneling, and typical Victorian molded plaster ceilings. In 1936, Wokefield Park became St Benedict's Approved School and increased in size to accommodate workshops and staff housing.

Today, Wokefield Park is owned by De Vere Group, a hotel company that utilizes historic houses for conferences, business meetings, holidays, or golf breaks. Weddings are popular at Wokefield Park, as are large conferences and events held by companies such as MBW and KPMG. The mansion building at Wokefield Park has 87 rooms, while the nearby executive center, which began as a farmhouse servicing the mansion, has 222 rooms. There are another three buildings on the Wokefield Park site that offer bedrooms or conference space for guests.

Wokefield Park is also known for its 18-hole golf course, which was designed by Jonathan Gaunt in 1996. Other facilities available to visitors include gyms, swimming pools, saunas, and a range of outdoor activities such as archery, laser tag, and Segway tours.

What makes Wokefield Park famous

Wokefield Park is famous for its rich history and stunning architecture that has been preserved and maintained over several centuries. As one of the most significant country houses in Berkshire, Wokefield Park's design is typical of 18th-century country houses and is notable for its Doric Stone portico and decorative Roman cement facing. The mansion's interiors are equally impressive, with a molded handrail and twisted balusters on the 18th-century stairway, typical Victorian molded plaster ceilings, and contemporary fireplaces. The house's vaulted cellar is thought to date back to Edmund Plowden's ownership in the late 16th century, adding to its historical significance. Wakefield Park's impact on architecture is considerable, with the house serving as an excellent example of Georgian design, and its influence can be seen in many other buildings throughout the region.

Visitors' Information

As a hotel, conference center, and wedding venue, Wokefield Park is not open to the public unless they are visitors staying at the house or using the conference facilities.

ALNWICK CASTLE
An Iconic Castle in Northumberland

Key Facts about Alnwick Castle

- A castle was built on the site of Alnwick Castle as early as 1096, following the Norman Conquest.
- The castle has been the seat of the Percy family since 1309, and members of the family still live in a part of the castle today.
- After Windsor Castle, Alnwick Castle is the second largest inhabited castle in England and is visited by over 800,000 people per year.
- Alnwick Castle has become famous in the 21st century for its use as a filming location for the Harry Potter films.

Overlooking the lush green meadows of the banks of the River Aln and dominating the small town of Alnwick in Northumberland is the vast medieval fortress of Alnwick Castle. The stark and dramatic exterior of the castle, the site of various battles and sieges throughout the Middle Ages, contrasts with its opulent Victorian interiors and landscaped gardens that have led to Alnwick Castle being dubbed 'Britain's answer to Versailles.'

The early history of Alnwick Castle is fraught with plots, rebellions, sieges, and surrenders. The castle was first built in 1096 by Yves de Vescy, the Baron of Alnwick. Due to its location close to the Scottish border, the castle was repeatedly besieged by the Scots until Henry Percy, the 1st Baron of Percy, purchased the barony and castle in 1309. Henry and his son, the 2nd Baron of Percy, commissioned ambitious building works that transformed Alnwick Castle from a modest stone castle into the major palace fortress it is today.

The 1st and 2nd Barons of Percy created a prestigious and sprawling castle in the form of an outer bailey enclosing a massive shell keep that comprises a cluster of towers set around an inner courtyard. This ambitious architectural project, balancing the requirements of a military stronghold with the needs of a high society family, is said to have inspired succeeding castle renovations throughout the 14th century.

The Percy family are descended from a great-grandmother of Charlemagne and, throughout the Middle Ages, were the most powerful lords in Northern England. The grandson of the 1st Baron of Percy, Henry the 1st Earl of Northumberland, played a major role in dethroning King Richard II. Later, he rebelled against King Henry IV, who threatened to destroy Alnwick Castle in retaliation but, thankfully, never did. The castle was surrendered to Henry IV in 1403.

Throughout the bloody and prolonged War of the Roses, Alnwick Castle was captured by Lancastrian forces numerous times. Once the House of York and the House of Lancaster were finally united by the marriage of Henry VII and Elizabeth of York, the military importance of Alnwick Castle waned. What followed was a period of abandonment succeeded by a complete restoration. While the appearance of the exterior of the building was not altered, the interiors were completely transformed. In the 1760s, the foremost architect of the time, Robert Adams, was employed to renovate the castle interiors using a Strawberry Hill gothic style, completely at odds with his usual neoclassical work.

Less than 100 years later, the 4th Duke of Northumberland demolished all of Robert Adams's interiors, transforming the castle into an ambitious project that involved transporting the castle's state rooms from the outer bailey into the keep. A grand staircase was assembled leading to the staterooms, which became some of the finest and most intricately decorated Victorian rooms in England. At an estimated cost of £250,000, the 4th Duke hired Anthony Salvin to construct the Prudhoe Tower, new staterooms, a kitchen, and a new layout for the inner ward.

Next, he employed Italian Luigi Canina and his assistant Giovanni Montiroli to decorate these new additions in a decadent

Italian style. The Florentine carver Anton Bulletti was also hired to train 27 local men in the ways of Italian craftsmanship. The creation of Alnwick Castle's state rooms, its finely carved cornices, picture frames, and furniture was the work of these men, and the skills they learned on the job led to what became known as the Alnwick School of Craftsmanship.

The upper guard chamber and library at Alnwick Castle hold treasures by artists such as Titian, Canaletto, van Dyck, and Sebastian del Piombo, as well as busts of Bacon, Newton, and Shakespeare. The saloon and drawing room feature intricately carved geometrical ceilings as well as grand fireplaces and pietra dura cabinets imported from Italy. The 1st Duke and Duchess of Northumberland are immortalized in a pair of paintings hung over the fireplace in the dining room, casting their eyes over an extensive and perfectly conserved Meissen dinner service.

Today, the current duke and his family are still residents in the castle, but they only occupy a small part of the sprawling building. During the summer months, a portion of the castle is open to the public, and special exhibitions are held in three of the castle's towers, mostly on the subjects of military history, archaeology, and classical history.

What Makes Alnwick Castle Famous?

Alnwick Castle is one of the most visited stately homes in the UK. The size of the castle and the fact that it has remained relatively unchanged since it was dramatically extended in the 14th century has made it one of the finest medieval castles in the country. The Duchess of Northumberland Jane Percy established the Alnwick Gardens in 2003, which feature a viewing fountain, tree house, cafe, and 'poisoned garden.' Alnwick Castle has achieved worldwide fame in the 21st century as the filming location for both the exterior and interior of Hogwarts School of Magic in the Harry Potter series of films.

Featured in TV and Film

- Downton Abbey (2010) TV Series
- Harry Potter and the Chamber of Secrets (2002)
- Harry Potter and the Philosopher's Stone (2001)
- Elizabeth (1998)
- Antiques Roadshow (1997) TV Series
- Robin Hood Prince of Thieves (1991)
- Mary Queen of Scots (1971)
- Beckett (1964)
- Prince Valiant (1954)

Further Research

- James McDonald (2012) Alnwick Castle: Home of the Duke and Duchess of Northumberland
- Colin Shrimpton (1999) Great Houses: Alnwick Castle
- Dan Jones (2013) The Plantaganets
- Duke of Northumberland and Richard A. Lomas (1999) Power in the Land: The Percys
- Richard A. Lomas (2007) The Fall of the House of Percy

Visiting Information

Alnwick Castle and Gardens is open to the public from March until October between the hours of 10.00 am and 5.30 pm. Thirty-five miles from Newcastle International Airport and 35 miles from the Port of Tyne, Alnwick Gardens are accessible by air and sea. If traveling by car, Alnwick Castle is less than a mile from major motorway A1, and the property's postcode is NE66 1YU. Alnwick is connected to the city of Newcastle Upon Tyne by buses X15 and X18, and the East Coast mainline train from London to Edinburgh stops at Alnmouth, which is four miles from Alnwick. We suggest taking a short taxi or bus from the train station. For more detailed information, view the website www.alnwickcastle.com

KINGSTON LACY
A Beautiful Italianate Country House in Dorset

Key Facts about Kingston Lacy

- Kingston Lacy is located near Wimborne Minster in Dorset, England.
- Originally constructed in 1663, it was the seat of the Bankes family for three centuries.
- Kingston Lacy is now the property of the National Trust.

Often referred to as an 'explorer' and 'adventurer,' William John Bankes lived his life with such vigor that Byron referred to him as 'the father of all mischiefs.' Kingston Lacy, a glorious Italianate country house originally built in the 17th century, is a monument to Banker's adventures. Following his tragic exile from his own country due to 'homosexual acts, ' Bankes continued to give instructions on the decoration and renovation of his house, making Kingston Lacy one of the most enchanting houses in England with one of the most poignant legacies.

The building of Kingston Hall was commissioned by Ralph Bankes and designed and built by Sir Roger Pratt between the years 1663 and 1665. The grounds on which Kingston Hall stood were originally part of a royal estate, and during medieval times, the original house, built sometime around the 14th century, was used as a hunting lodge. By the 16th century, the house was uninhabitable and was eventually sold to Sir John Bankes, Attorney General to King Charles I and father of Ralph Bankes, in 1636.

The Bankes' main property, Corfe Castle, was destroyed by Parliamentarian sieges during the English Civil War. Sir John was killed for his loyalty to the throne. In 1645, parliament voted to demolish Corfe Castle, so the remaining family put their time and fortune into the building of Kingston Hall. By the time Kingston Hall passed through the generations and fell into the hands of the infamous William Bankes, the Bankes family fortune was vast, and their tastes refined. William Bankes was not content with the red brick house his ancestors had envisioned and employed his Charles Barry to re-envision the house as a grey stone palazzo-style mansion, henceforth to be known as Kingston Lacy.

Kingston Lacy was transformed between the years of 1835 and 1838. Its facade was faced with Chilmark Stone, a new entrance was created by exposing the basement level of the house, and a tall chimney was added to each corner. The already extensive estate containing 12 acres of formal gardens and 360 acres of parklands was further improved, and miles of beech tree avenues were planted along the Blandford Road.

During the mid-nineteenth century, William Bankes was the epitome of the Byronic European excess. Wealthy and aristocratic, he traveled widely in Europe and the Middle East, collecting antiquities to take home to Kingston Lacy. During his lifetime, Bankes amassed the largest individual collection of Egyptian antiquities in the world, most of which are still on display in the basement of Kingston Lacy.

Contentiously, many of these objects were taken from the workmen's village in the Valley of the Kings. Even more shockingly, Kingston Lacy is home to the Philea Obelisk, an engraved stone structure featuring both Egyptian and Greek characters that played a key role in the eventual decipherment of Egyptian hieroglyphics. It took six years to transport the obelisk back from Egypt to Dorset, and there it stands, eroding and mourning the loss of its mirror image left behind where it belongs on its Egyptian temple island.

It is not just the basement and grounds of Kingston Lacy that are replete with treasure, however. Everything about the house is impressive. The white Carrara marble staircase features three statues by Carlo Marochetti depicting Sir John, Lady Bankes, and their beloved King Charles I. The doors to the drawing room are another particular treat, with carved marble architraves made in Verona. On the wall of the Library hang the keys to Corfe Castle, vigorously defended by the Bankes family during the English Civil War.

For art lovers, the collection of paintings hung on the many walls of Kingston Lacy is its triumph. In the dining room, already luxuriant with its intricately carved boxwood doors, hangs Sebastian del Piombo's unfinished Judgement of Solomon. The saloon was renovated by Robert Brettingham in the 18th century and bore all of the hallmarks of his style. Here hang Banke's two greatest acquisitions, portraits of Maria Di Antonio Serra and Maria Grimaldi by Reubens. Other fine works by artists such as Titian, Rembrandt, van Dyck, Lely, and Kneller adorn the other rooms of the house, including the state bedrooms, which once saw a visit from Kaiser Wilhelm II.

In 1841, William Bankes was embroiled in a scandal with the accusation of committing homosexual acts, leaving him vulnerable to a trial and possible execution. Bankes fled the country for Italy, where he sought refuge from the scandal but, for the next fourteen years, was unable to leave Kingston Lacy behind. Through his sister, Lady Falmouth, William Bankes directed further building works, designed interiors, and continued to send back precious items he collected abroad.

While officially, Bankes never returned to the UK; family legend has it that in 1854, with his death rapidly approaching, Bankes made one final secret visit to the one true love of his life, Kingston Lacy. Following Banke's death, the house passed through generations of the Bankes family but was notoriously inaccessible to the public. It wasn't until 1981 that current owner Ralph Bankes, seven times great-grandson of the original Kingston Lacy Sir Ralph Bankes, bequeathed the house, estates, and collections to the National Trust so the public could finally take a look inside.

What makes Kingston Lacy Famous?

The collections at Kingston Lacy are some of the finest and most historically significant of any country house in England. The archaeological finds on display in the basement of Kingston Lacy, as well as the famous Philea obelisk, are globally significant. The fascinating life story of William Bankes, the 'father of mischief,' and his poignant end make Kingston Lacy the stuff of English aristocratic legend.

Anglotopia's Take

This one is another one of our frequent visits when we're spending time in Dorset. It's a beautiful Italianate house with lots of history and grounds to explore. It's closely connected with Corfe Castle, which used to be the family's home before it was ruined in the English Civil Wars (the keys to the castle are in one of the rooms). We're also quite fond of the cafe; while most National Trust cafes are pretty much the same, we've always had a lovely lunch here.

Further Research

- Viola Bankes and Pamela Watkins (1986) A Kingston Lacy Childhood
- The Exiled Collector: William Bankes And the Making of an English Country House by Anne Sebba

Visiting Information

Kingston Lacy House is open to the public from March to October between the hours of 11 am and 5 pm, with special opening hours during the Christmas holiday season. The gardens and parks are open year-round. Kingston Lacy is located in Dorset and has the postcode BH21 4EA. It is just 12 miles from Bournemouth Airport and 91 miles from Heathrow. By car from Heathrow, take the M3 and M27 to the A31 and continue until you reach Dorset. From Bournemouth, take the B3073 to the B3082 Blandford to Wimborne Road and follow the brown tourist signs to the property. Trains are available from the nearby town of Poole, and buses are available from both Poole and Bournemouth. For more information, view the website www.nationaltrust.org.uk/kingston-lacy

KNOLE HOUSE
The Iconic Home of the Sackville Family

Key Facts about Knole House

- Knole House is located in the small town of Sevenoaks in West Kent, England.
- Knole House was built in 1456 and originally belonged to the Archbishop of Canterbury at the time, Thomas Bourchier.
- The house has been owned by the Sackville family from 1605 to the present day through thirteen generations.

Knole House, located in the town of Sevenoaks in West Kent, England, is an impressive and historic estate that has stood for over 600 years. The mansion was built in the 15th century and has since been expanded and remodeled, making it one of the largest and most imposing houses in the country. Knole House has a rich and fascinating history, having been the home of several notable families throughout the centuries, including the Archbishop of Canterbury, the Sackville family, and the Earls of Dorset. Today, the house is open to the public and is a popular tourist attraction, offering visitors a glimpse into the grandeur and opulence of England's aristocratic past.

An old manor already existed on the site of Knole House when, in 1456, the archbishop of Canterbury set about building a palace fit for a man of the cloth. Despite the size of the mansion he created over the next thirty years, the archbishop did little to make the exterior of the building attractive or impressive. Instead, Knole

House's charm is located within its walls as over the next 100 years, the house's interiors were repeatedly renovated and refurbished by successive owners. During the Reformation in 1538, the house was plucked from Cranmer by King Henry VIII, whose daughter Elizabeth I passed the house on to her cousins, the Sackville family, later Dukes of Dorset.

Knole House is thought to have been conceived as a 'Calendar House', which once boasted the pleasingly Gregorian statistics of 365 rooms, 52 staircases, 12 entrances, and 7 courtyards. The central gatehouse of Knole House opens into Green Court, which then leads to a second gatehouse flanked by two grand galleries leading to Stone Court, the ceremonial court fronting the essential Great Hall. Rooms are set around seven round courtyards with beguiling names like Green, Stone, Water, and Pheasant in a typical Tudor layout.

As soon as The 1st Earl of Dorset came into possession of the house in 1605, he set about completely rebuilding its interiors, and it is at his hands that Knole House was given its crowning glory, the Great Staircase. An intoxicating example of the English Renaissance, the staircase is dominated by Greek-style marble columns while delicate murals depict the Four Ages of Man, the Social Virtues, and the Five Senses. At the same time the staircase was constructed, the 1st Earl added a famously striking Jacobean screen to the Great Hall. The upstairs suites at Knole House are renowned for their palatial interiors as well as their numbers. Several magnificent suites exist at Knole House, each housing a treasure trove of furnishings fit for, and in some cases used by, a King. The Venetian Ambassadors Room contains a state bed, chairs, stools, and tapestries commissioned for a visit by James II in 1688.

The hand of the 1st Earl of Dorset can clearly be seen in the Ballroom of Knole House; the chimney-piece was carved by Cornelius Cure and is one of the best examples of English Rennaisance sculpture in England, and the walls are lined with full-length portraits of the Sackvilles by artists Larkin, van Dyck, and Kneller. And yet, the King's Suite is surely the most impressive of all. Two closets, a lavatory, and a dressing room lead to the King's Bedroom, which is adorned in such precious fabrics and furnishings it must be kept in low light at all times. Items of the decor, such as the silver filigree mirrors and silver toilet set, are said to have been sent to James II directly from France.

A wander around the state rooms open to the public at Knole House will reward visitors with a glimpse of paintings by Van Dyke, Gainsborough, and Sir Joshua Reynolds. Reynold's portrait subjects include Samuel Johnson, Oliver Goldsmith, and the Chinese page boy, Wang-y-tong, who was one of the first Chinese people to visit England and was taken into the Sackville household in 1776 as a page to one of John Sackville's mistresses.

Of the many Sackville descendants to have lived at Knole House, none can be more fascinating than Vita Sackville-West, a writer who wrote Knole and the Sackville (1922). Vita Sackville-West was both lover and muse to writer Virginia Woolf, whose novel Orlando (1928) is said to be written as a partly biographical, partly fantastical account of Sackville-West's life. One of the most touching love letters ever written, Orlando tells the story of a gender-switching individual who has lived for over 300 years.

Today, Knole House is mostly cared for by the National Trust, with more than half of the house still owned by the Sackville-West family. Certain rooms are open to the public, and projects supported by the Heritage Lottery Fund are ongoing to conserve the showrooms and build adequate facilities for the conservation work.

What Makes Knole House Very Famous?

One of the largest country houses in England to have been owned by the same aristocratic family through thirteen generations, Knole House is the epitome of old English houses. If these walls could talk, they would no doubt have spun a web of tales that could rival Virginia Woolf's novel Orlando in their tantalizing strangeness. Providing a bed for many a King and Queen to rest over the years, Knole House is like a stately old ship that has weathered many a storm and yet kept its treasures safely within.

Anglotopia's Take

Kent is filled with stately homes and castles (thanks to its proximity to London), so there is no shortage of things to see when visiting. Knole should be at the top of your list. The house is simply packed with history going back almost one thousand years.

Featured in TV and Film

- Hunters of the Khari (2006)
- The Other Boleyn Girl (2008)
- Burke and Hare (2010)
- Sherlock Holmes: A Game of Shadows (2011)
- Pirates of the Caribbean: On Stranger Tides (2011)

Further Research

- Vita Sackville-West (1922) Knole and the Sackvilles
- Robert Sackville-West (2011) Inheritance: The Story of Knole and the Sackvilles
- Knole National Trust Guidebook (1998)
- Baron Lionel Sackville-West (2012) Knole House: Its State Rooms, Pictures and Antiquities

Visiting Information

Knole's 1,000-acre park is open to the public all year round, but the showrooms are only open between the hours of 10 am and 4 pm from April to September. Knole House is located just 26 miles from Gatwick Airport. If traveling by car, take the M23 to the A25 in Kent and follow brown tourist signs to Knole House. If coming from the north, use the M25 and exit at exit 5 for Sevenoaks. From the south, use the A21 for Sevenoaks. The postcode for the property is TN13 1HU. The London Underground will take you from central London to London Charing Cross, London Bridge, and London Victoria, from which you can get overground trains to Sevenoaks.

The walk from Sevenoaks Train Station takes around 15 minutes, or alternatively, take a taxi. For more detailed information, visit the website www.nationaltrust.org.uk/knole.

BERKELEY CASTLE
A Medieval Gothic Wonder

Key Facts About Berkeley Castle

- Berkeley Castle is located south of the town of Berkley in Gloucestershire, England.
- A Grade I listed building, Berkeley Castle, was built around 1067 following the Norman Conquest.
- The castle has been the property of the Berkley family from the 12th century to the present day, apart from a short period of Royal ownership during Tudor times.

For anyone who still remembers their English History lessons, Berkeley Castle is a place of horror: a medieval gothic castle famed for being the setting of the grisly murder of Edward II and home to many a ghost with unfinished business. Remarkably, Berkeley Castle has belonged to the same family since its first incarnation in the 11th century and is today not haunted or horrifying in the slightest, but a popular location for weddings and other special events.

There are many 19th-century English castles built in the picturesque, medieval-gothic style of earlier times, but Berkeley Castle is the real thing. The first motte-and-bailey castle was built at Berkeley in Gloucestershire in 1067, just after the Norman Conquest, by William FitzOsbern. The castle passed through three generations of this family before passing to Robert Fitzharding in 1153, the first of the branch of the Berkeley family that owns Berkeley Castle today.

Over the next few decades, the castle was rebuilt and extended following a royal charter from King Henry II, who saw Berkeley Castle as a defensive stronghold in the protection of Severn Estuary, Welsh border, and Bristol to Gloucester Road. The former motte was replaced by Fitzharding with a circular shell keep, and later, the curtain wall was added.

In 1327, Berkeley Castle became notorious as the site of the imprisonment and murder of King Edward II. Various accounts of this ghastly murder exist, but in the most cited version, Edward was killed not by his jailer, Lord Thomas de Berkeley, but by Edward II's own wife, Isabella of France, and her lover Mortimer. Within the King's Gallery, a room dedicated to the unfortunate King's stay, there is a large hole that leads down into the dungeon. It is said that the corpses of both men and animals were thrown down this hole in the hope that any prisoners in the room would die of either disease or asphyxiation brought on by the fumes of the rotting corpses. It seems Edward survived his imprisonment in this disgusting room only to be stabbed to death with a hot poker while sleeping in his bed. With King Edward II out of the way, Isabella's lover Mortimer took the throne only to be ousted four years later by Isabella's legitimate son Edward III.

Following King Edward II's death, his body lay in state at Berkeley Castle for a month in the Chapel of St John and was later escorted by Thomas de Berkeley to Gloucester Abbey for burial. Although accused of being involved in the murder, Thomas de Berkeley was later cleared of all charges. With this unpleasantness behind him, Thomas de Berkeley spent the years between 1340 and 1361 expanding and improving his castle.

Within the inner bailey, backing onto the curtain wall, Thomas de Berkeley created a series of domestic rooms. The picture gallery, dining room, and kitchen are all wonderful examples of 14th-century interiors, but it is the Great Hall that remains the core of the castle. Within the structure of the Great Hall's roof, visitors can see the finest example of what is known as the 'Berkeley arch,' an architectural quirk that consists of both curved and straight edges. The Great Hall also features a 15th-century screen with original paintwork and a portrait of Admiral Sir George Berkeley by Gainsborough.

The great staircase leads up to the staterooms, which include an original chapel, now used as a morning room, with wooden vaulted ceilings and a frieze featuring a 14th-century translation of the bible from Latin to Norman French. The long and small drawing rooms have survived intact since the 14th century. Now adorned in tapestries and rugs of the Victorian Gothic era, the long drawing room features a portrait of Mary Cole, who married the 5th Earl of Berkeley in secret. Mary's working-class heritage and contests over the legitimacy of the secret wedding led to a trial over their children's claim to the castle. While it was ruled that the eldest son could not keep the Earldom, he did keep Berkeley, and the castle remains in the Berkeley family to this day.

A final feature of Berkeley Castle that deserves mention is the breach in the castle walls. During the siege of 1645, Parliamentarian forces led by Colonel Thomas Rainsborough fired cannons at point-blank range into the keep and outer bailey of Alnwick Castle. An Act of Parliament following the battle decreed that the Berkeleys could retain ownership of the castle but must never repair the breach in the castle walls, and they never have.

Why is Berkeley Castle Famous?

Being the supposed site of the murder of King Edward II is enough to secure Berkeley Castle's place in most of the great tomes of English History, as well as make it a sought-after location for our nation's many Haunted House reality TV shows. But Berkeley Castle is also renowned for the remarkable feat of remaining in the same family since the 12th century and the preservation of its mostly 14th-century architecture. Berkeley Castle is one of the most impressive medieval castles in the country, described by historical writer Simon Jenkins as Britain's own 'rose-red city half as old as time.'

Featured in TV and Film

- Wolf Hall (2015) TV mini-series
- The Other Boleyn Girl (2008)
- Castle in the Country (2005) TV series
- Just Visiting (2001)
- History of Britain (2000) TV mini-series

Further Research

- Vita Sackville-West and Nicholas McCann (1997) Berkeley Castle (Great Houses)
- Dan Jones (2013) The Plantagenets
- Ian Mortimer (2009) A Time Traveller's Guide to Medieval Britain

Visiting Information

Berkeley Castle is open to the public between the hours of 11 am and 5 pm on Sundays, Mondays, Tuesdays, and Wednesdays from 1st April to 29th October. Berkeley Castle is accessible from both Bristol and London Airports. If traveling by car, use the M4 motorway, exit at junction 20, and take the M5 north to Junction 14. Head north on the A38 following signs for Berkeley and then brown tourist attraction signs to Berkeley Castle. The property's postcode is GL13 9PJ. You can also take the train from London Paddington to Bristol Meads or Bristol Parkway, change for Cam and Dursley station, and then take a 15-minute taxi to the castle. For more detailed information, visit the website www.berkeley-castle.com.

WENTWORTH WOODHOUSE
Britain's Largest Stately Home Facade

Key Facts about Wentworth Woodhouse

- Wentworth Woodhouse is located in the village of Wentworth, 5 miles from Rotherham in South Yorkshire, England.
- The original house was built by Thomas Wentworth in the 1630s but was completely rebuilt in the 1720s by Thomas Watson-Wentworth.
- Wentworth Woodhouse has been owned by descendants of Thomas Watson-Wentworth since 1725 until it passed through marriage to the Earls Fitzwilliam. Since the 1980s, the house has had various private owners and has been sold to a new owner as recently as 2015. It's now owned by a trust and managed by the National Trust.

One of the great Whig political palaces of the 18th century, Wentworth Woodhouse is the largest country house in England, with a façade that stretches over 600 feet. There are over 300 rooms in Wentworth Woodhouse, rooms that have been inhabited over the years by the influential Watson-Wentworth dynasty and, later, the Earls Fitzwilliam. Recently, the house described by Arthur Lee as a 'standing astonishing witness to the commonplace grandeur of the 18th century' was controversially sold to a company from Hong Kong for a reported £ 8 million.

Little is known of the first house that stood on the site of Wentworth Woodhouse other than that it was a Jacobean structure built by Thomas Wentworth, 1st Earl of Strafford, in the 1630s. Sadly, the first earl had little time to enjoy his house as he was sacrificed by King Charles I and executed by Parliamentarians in 1641.

In 1723, the next Thomas Wentworth, later the Marquis

of Rockingham, inherited the house and, within two years, had begun to rebuild it completely. The brick-built, western front of Wentworth Woodhouse was conceived in the Baroque style and was the handiwork of a local builder and architect, Ralph Tunnicliffe. The Baroque style was already out of fashion, though, and before this part of the new house was even finished, the current Earl's grandson, Thomas Watson-Wentworth, commissioned the building of a completely new east range, which was, in reality, a much larger house built back-to-back with the existing one.

The design of the new house is thought to have been based on Colen Campbell's Wanstead House. Featuring a façade that is 606 feet long, it was, and may still be, the largest house in England. The front of the house has nineteen bays with an entrance portico accessible from a central double flight of steps. One explanation given for the monstrous proportions of this house is that they were the result of a boastful rivalry between the Stainborough and Watson branches of the Wentworth family, instigated by terms of inheritance that were not satisfactory to both parties.

Before the building began, plans for the new house were vetted by Henry Flitcroft and his 'Burlington's Committee of Taste.' As a result, Flitcroft swooped in on Tunnicliffe's plan and was employed as the new architect. Over the next decade, Flitcroft not only built the east front but revised and enlarged Tunnicliffe's existing west front and added wings. Looking out onto the giardano secret and walled kitchen garden, the west front was intended for family use whereas the east front was a magnificent declaration of the Westcroft's social and political ambitions.

Charles Wentworth-Watson, 2nd Marquess of Rockingham, inherited Wentworth Woodhouse in the mid-1800s and, in 1765, 1766, and 1782, enjoyed brief spells as Prime Minister. Charles Wentworth employed an architect, John Carr of York, in the 1980s and added corner pavilions to each of the east wings and an extra story to parts of the East Front.

Over the succeeding years, the owners of Wentworth Woodhouse filled the rooms within the house with a staggering collection of art and sculpture. In the 19th century Wentworth Woodhouse ranked with Harewood and Castle Howard as one of the greatest houses of the North. Notably, the Pillard Hall featured designs for panels contributed by James 'Athenian' Stuart. A painting by Stubbs of the famous racehorse Whistlejacket hangs in one of the rooms, as does Hogarth's Rockingham family group. Paintings by van Dyck, Reynolds, and Lely can also be found on the walls at Wentworth, with subjects ranging from kings and queens to Strafford. The second Marquess even planned to add a sculpture gallery to Wentworth and had Joseph Nollekens create four marbles for pride of place, but the galley never came to fruition, and the sculptures can now be found at the J. Paul Getty Museum in Paris, and Victoria and Albert Museum in London.

Wentworth Woodhouse was inherited through marriage by the Earls Fitzwilliam and remained with the family until 1979, when it passed to the heirs of the earls. The house fell into disrepair in the 20th century, during which time a large quantity of coal was discovered on the estate's land. Mining did take place around the estate in the 1950s, and in the 1960s and 70s, the house was let to Lady Mabel College of Physical Education and later Sheffield Hallam University.

In the last few centuries, Wentworth Woodhouse has passed through various private owners. Most recently, the house and estate were sold to a Hong Kong-based company for £8 million. The bid was accepted over a National Trust bid to save the house 'for the nation.' The house is now owned by a preservation trust, and it's being managed by the National Trust.

What Makes Wentworth Woodhouse so Famous?

Its claim to having the longest continuous façade in the country, its magnificent 18th-century Palladian style, and over 300 rooms full of treasure make Wentworth Woodhouse one of the most splendid houses in England. Besides its epic scale, Wentworth Woodhouse is famous for being the home of some of the most influential Whig politicians of the 18th and 19th centuries, even being inhabited by a Prime Minster at one point. Its unique Baroque west front, Palladian east front structure, and the fact that it's been closed to the public for over sixty years have made Wentworth

Woodhouse one of the most fascinating private houses.

In 2017, Wentworth Woodhouse was sold to a Hong Kong-based company named Wentworth Woodhouse Preservation Trust Ltd. for a reported £8 million. The trust aims to restore the house and open it to the public as a tourist attraction and events venue. The National Trust has been working with the new preservation trust to open the house up to the public.

In Film and TV

- Wives and Daughters (1999)
- The Thirteenth Tale (2013)
- Mr. Turner (2014)
- Jonathan Strange & Mr Norrell (2015)

Further Research

- Catherine Bailey (2008) Black Diamonds: The Rise and Fall of an English Dynasty
- John Martin Robinson (2014) Requisitioned: The British Country House in the Second World War
- Heather Ewen (2006) Wentworth, My Wentworth

Visiting Information

If you'd like to visit Wentworth Woodhouse, you can check their website for tour information and ticket prices. They offer different types of tours, including guided tours of the house and gardens, as well as self-guided tours. The house is located in the village of Wentworth, which is about 5 miles from Rotherham in South Yorkshire, England. You can reach the village by car or take public transportation via bus or train. View the website https://wentworthwoodhouse.org.uk/ for more information.

ST MICHAEL'S MOUNT
Cornwall's Island of Giants

Key facts about St Michael's Mount

- St Michael's Mount is a small island, monastery, and castle located in Mount's Bay, Cornwall, England.
- A priory was first built on the site in 1135, and the castle and surrounding buildings were built over the succeeding seven centuries.
- The Mount passed through many owners before Colonel St Aubyn bought it in 1659. His descendants owned and lived on the mount until 1954 when it was given to the National Trust.

A crumbling medieval monastery and sprawling castle sit atop an offshore island that's only accessible on foot during low tide. St Michael's Mount seems very much like the setting of a fairy tale. But the tumultuous Middle Ages, Henry VIII's dissolution of the monasteries, and more contemporary British crises such as World War II have made St Michael's Mount an important historical stronghold, scenic but strategic. Now, St Michael's Mount offers visitors a picturesque castle, well preserved but also much altered over the centuries, and elegant sub-tropical gardens with a pretty harbor below.

There is evidence that St Michael's Mount was inhabited at least as early as the Neolithic era (4000-2500 BCE years), and it may have been used as a trade port for continental tradesmen picking up Cornish tin bound for the Mediterranean during the first few centuries AD. Whether the Mount was the ancient port known as Ictus is unclear, but what we do know for certain is that Edward the Confessor gave the Mount to the Norman abbey of Mont Saint-

Michel in the year 1135. Benedictine monks from this abbey were invited to establish a priory in Cornwall, an invitation they accepted, and over the next few centuries, carefully and painstakingly built their church.

In 1425, the monks also laid a rough causeway that, at ebb tide, made the mount accessible on foot from the seaward side. The monks lived in peace for a number of years until St Michael's Mount became a strategic base for Perkin Warbeck, a pretender to the throne of King Henry VII. After Warbeck's failed rebellion during the War of the Roses, he sought refuge in St Michael's Mount with his notoriously beautiful wife Catherine, one of many women who thought they had married a king during these tumultuous times but never did become queen.

Following King Henry VIII's Dissolution of the Monasteries, St Michael's Mount was occupied by a number of crown-approved military governors who kept the fortified island in good shape and defended it against Parliamentarian forces who tried to take it in 1642. Their victory was short-lived as St Michael's Mount was surrendered to Parliamentarian forces in 1646 and fell under the command of John St Aubyn, a Parliamentary colonel who was nominated governor and began to adapt the existing building on the mount, part monastery, part castle, into a residence. Descendants of John St Aubyn, the Lords St Levan, live at St Michael's Mount to this day and are responsible for the many architectural transformations the building has undergone.

Some parts of the medieval incarnation of St Michael's Mount remain, such as the gatehouse, the converted Lady Chapel, and the church and refectory with garrison quarters underneath. The church is thought to date back to the thirteenth century, and St Michael's chapel dates back to the fifteenth. What was initially the monastic refectory, built in the twelfth century, became the Tudor Great Hall and features a magnificent arch-braced roof. This roof was restored in the nineteenth century, at which point the room entered the third stage of its existence and became known as the Chevy Chase Room. This name comes from the incredible plaster friezes of hunting scenes that line its walls. A Jacobean oak table with a full set of monastic chairs completes the imposing effect.

The most revered room at St Michael's Mount is the old monastic Lady Chapel, which was gloriously converted into a drawing room during the mid-eighteenth century. With views from the north terrace of the very summit of the island, this carefully conserved Georgian treat has interiors in the style of Strawberry Hill Gothic, featuring pretty pale blue and white ornamentation and a significant landscape of the mount itself by artist Robert Opie.

The rest of the castle displays the old barracks and museum rooms. A number of other buildings can be found dotted around the castle, including a row of late nineteenth-century houses known as Elizabeth Terrace, some of which are occupied by castle employees, and the former stables, laundry, steward's house, and two former inns.

What Makes St Michael's Mount Very Famous?

St Michael's Mount is famous both for historical and mythical reasons. An important Benedictine priory used as a stronghold by a pretender king during the Wars of the Roses held for the King during the Civil War before being taken by a parliamentarian Colonel and machine-gunned during World War II, St Michael's Mount has seen its share of real-life warfare. But the mount also has an aura of mystery. They have made it the setting of the legend of Jack the Giant Killer and a filming location for various Dracula films. An iconic rocky island on the coast of Cornwall, St Michael's Mount has many stories to tell.

Anglotopia's Take

One of the hardest houses to get to in England, simply because of its distance from London in Cornwall, it also has the added bonus of being on its own island. Getting to the island is a challenge as it's based on the tides - you can either walk, take a boat, or a special truck that navigates the channel. Despite all this, it's well worth visiting. It's a very mythical and atmospheric place. Battered by the seas and the winds, it's no wonder the place is built of stone.

Don't miss an opportunity to visit. Eat your Wheaties, though; the climb from the harbor to the castle is quite strenuous!

Featured in TV and Film

- Dracula (1979)
- Never Say Never Again (1983)
- Johnny English (2003)
- Maria Mudhi and the Midas Box (2012)

Further Research

- James St Aubyn, A Personal Tour of St Michael's Mount
- McCabe, Helen (1988). Houses and Gardens of Cornwall.

Visiting Information

St Michael's Mount is open to the public, but the opening times are complicated and vary depending on day, month, and season, so it is best to visit the website www.stmichaelsmount.co.uk before you visit. When the tide is in, the Mount is accessible by one of St Michael's Mount's ferry boats, and when it's out, you can walk across the causeway. To get to St Michael's Mount by car, travel on the A30 to Penzance, then follow the signs for Marazion. There is ample car parking in a seafront car park. There is also an intercity train link to Penzance station, from which you can take a local bus or taxi to Marazion.

www.ingramcontent.com/pod-product-compliance
Lightning Source LLC
Chambersburg PA
CBHW032033150426
43194CB00006B/261